Hawley Smart

From Post to Finish

Vol. 3

Hawley Smart

From Post to Finish
Vol. 3

ISBN/EAN: 9783337346331

Printed in Europe, USA, Canada, Australia, Japan

Cover: Foto ©Thomas Meinert / pixelio.de

More available books at **www.hansebooks.com**

FROM POST TO FINISH

FROM POST TO FINISH

A Novel.

BY

HAWLEY SMART,

AUTHOR OF "BREEZIE LANGTON," "THE GREAT TONTINE," "AT FAULT,"
"HARD LINES," &c. &c.

"Looked as though the speed of thought
Were in his limbs: but he was wild,
Wild as the wild deer, and untaught."

IN THREE VOLUMES.

VOL. III.

LONDON—CHAPMAN AND HALL
LIMITED.
1884.

(All rights reserved.)

WESTMINSTER:
PRINTED BY NICHOLS AND SONS,
25, PARLIAMENT STREET.

CONTENTS

VOLUME III.

CHAP.	PAGE
I.—Gerald's Identity proclaimed	1
II.—Ellen consults John Thorndyke	20
III.—The Dancing Master proves incorrigible	38
IV.—Gerald visits York	55
V.—A Call in St. Leonard's Place	74
VI.—"Will you be my Wife?"	94
VII.—Poor old Dancer	110
VIII.—Cranley goes to the Hammer	133
IX.—Dollie turns Schoolmistress	150
X.—Stealing a Kiss	169
XI.—Going for the Gloves	191
XII.—At the Rutland Arms	209
XIII.—Getting at the Favourite	226
XIV.—The Cambridgeshire	247
XV.—Conclusion	270

FROM POST TO FINISH.

CHAPTER I.

GERALD'S IDENTITY PROCLAIMED.

WE are most of us blessed with spinster aunts. I am not speaking ironically of that acidulated maiden lady, who, in consideration of having money to leave behind her, deems herself entitled both to cross-examine us about our doings, and lecture us severely should they not meet her approval, but of one of those dear old ladies who are pleased with small attentions, who take the greatest interest in the careers of all the family, who keep up a desultory correspondence with every branch of it, and are always doing small kindnesses to some of "the failures" amongst us. They invariably know more about the family as a whole than any one, and are usually, in some occult way, among the first to hear of any good or evil that may have befallen us. Ellen Rockingham had an aunt of the latter type, whom she regarded as a real infliction. Aunt Mary, Mrs. Rockingham's elder sister, was a sweet-tempered chatty old lady, with a modest independence and a large circle of acquaintance, amongst whom she was extremely popular. Moving, as she did, from one country house to another, and living when in London in quiet apartments in the vicinity of Portman Square, she was always quite *au fait* with all the current topics of the day, to say nothing of its gossip. Ellen was one of the few people who didn't get on with

Aunt Mary, and the cause of discord was Ellen's extreme religious views. Miss Stacey was quite orthodox, but very conventional in her worship. The old lady was quite content with going to church once on the Sabbath, and deemed it no great sin to indulge in forty winks during the sermon. She was quiet and unostentatious in her little charities, and perhaps did no great good in her life, but then she assuredly did many little kindnesses and no harm. Aunt Mary a little laughed at Ellen's night-schools and plans for the elevation of the bucolic mind, and thought that the Cranley people infinitely preferred their Christmas coals and blankets to drowsy discourses, and the shrewd practical help in the time of trouble of the late rector to the methodistical teaching and stern rebukes for improvidence that the present incumbent so delighted to administer. Of course Aunt Mary was right. Humanity does prefer a shilling and a kindly word to the shilling with the addenda of a severe lecture on the want of thrift that necessitates the need of it.

Now, Aunt Mary, in the expansiveness of her nature, when she heard of Alister Rockingham's death and the ruin that followed, had written promptly to her sister, and proposed that she and Ellen should make their home with her, a proposition which was kindly but firmly rejected. Still, Aunt Mary naturally took the keenest interest in the fallen fortunes of her sister. Some of the sunniest days of her life had been passed at Cranley, and she had entertained a most sincere affection for her brother-in-law. That Aunt Mary maintained a constant correspondence with St. Leonard's Place may easily be imagined, and she was therefore fully informed of Gerald's mysterious disappearance. She knew how uneasy his mother and sister were about him, but what she did not know was the change his father's death had wrought in Gerald. The last time she saw her nephew he had been a bright, laughter-loving boy, but the stern compulsion of earning his own living, and the knowledge that his mother and sister must depend upon him for those luxuries which were almost necessities for women brought up as they had been, had hardened his character and transformed him at one bound into a man. The small income derived from the few thousands settled on Mrs. Rockingham at her marriage was all that she and Ellen had left to them, and Gerald was very anxious to supplement that to some extent.

Mixing a good deal in society, Miss Stacey was not very long before she heard the mysterious Jim Forrest talked about. People, indeed, began to be very full of this little romance after Goodwood. From the club smoking-rooms the story of the gentleman who had turned professional jockey speedily spread all through the London world, and many curious eyes were bent on the lad's dark face from among the brilliant throng that crowded the Grand Stand at the great Ducal meeting. Still, Jim escaped recognition on that occasion, but the attention that had now been drawn to him made it, as Farrington had warned him, quite impossible that he could do so much longer.

Ere the October Meetings were over at Newmarket he had been recognised by some Yorkshire gentlemen as young Gerald Rockingham, and the fact was soon noised all over the heath. The first intimation Gerald received that his *incognito* was at an end came from Lord Whitby. The news had reached the ears of that sporting but choleric old peer, and, happening to encounter Gerald shortly afterwards in the Birdcage, he astonished him not a little by holding out his hand, and exclaiming:

"I shall be proud to make your acquaintance, Mr. Rockingham. I knew your poor father well, and a better, kinder-hearted fellow never breathed. Gad! I admire your pluck, and, by Jove, you're likely to do what neither your father nor myself ever did—make money out of racing."

"I had to do something for myself, Lord Whitby," replied Gerald, as he shook hands, "and bar ride and shoot there seemed nothing I could do. I have done pretty well so far."

"Pretty well! I should think you had. The way you got Pibroch home at Goodwood would have been a credit to any of the old hands. Damme, I'll give you a turn myself before long. I can trust you because you are one of us, but for all that don't back your mount when you don my colours. My horses never can win somehow."

"Jim Forrest" thanked his lordship,

but for all that he did not particularly covet any of his riding. The irascible peer was notorious on the turf for his persistent bad luck, and his violent outbursts of temper in consequence. It was not the money, for he was enormously wealthy, and, to do him justice, nobody cared less about money than Lord Whitby, but he did hate being beaten. In the first tempest of his wrath at defeat—and horses will at times fail to do what is expected of them—he was wont to cast round for some scapegoat upon whom the cause of his disappointment might be properly fathered. Obviously his trainer and jockey stood out as the proper recipients of his ever strongly expressed feelings on such occasions, and no man on the turf had changed his trainers and jockeys so often as Lord Whitby. It struck Jim at once that a ride on one of his lordship's nameless horses might be productive of much unpleasantness, albeit he had done his very best by his mount. His not naming his colts was another idiosyncracy of the hot-tempered though kind-hearted nobleman.

That the mysterious Jim Forrest is none other than the son of Alister Rockingham, who died a ruined man at the commencement of the year, stricken to death by his terrible losses over the Phaeton Leger, is a tale that spreads like wildfire through the clubs and midst country houses, and it is not long before Aunt Mary, sojourning in one of these latter, is made aware of it, her informant having no suspicion that Miss Stacey was the aunt of this young Centaur who had just appeared above the turf horizon. Aunt Mary was thunderstruck, she hardly knew for some hours what to think of it. That a Rockingham should be getting his living in such fashion seemed terrible in the old lady's eyes, but at the same time she could not but admire the way in which her featherpated nephew had met the shock of disaster; and then again Aunt Mary had lived too much in the horse-loving county and amongst racing men not to feel a wee bit proud of his deeds of " derring-do " in the saddle. No need to laugh at the word, though it is only the initiated of the racecourse who comprehend the nerve, head, and hands it requires to come round Tattenham Corner " on the rails."

Aunt Mary, on the receipt of this news, hurried up to her bedroom to think it all out. Firstly, had Mrs. Rockingham and Ellen the faintest idea of what Gerald was doing — it was some weeks since she had heard from them; and secondly, what were they all to do about it? That Gerald had taken his life into his own hands, and was little likely to listen to what kith or kin said concerning the manner of it, was a thing that Aunt Mary had no conception of. The good soul thought that she would have to assist at a little family counsel, consisting of herself, her sister, and her niece, at which, whether it was possible for Gerald to continue this—well, she would call it eccentric freak — might be calmly debated; and, actuated by that impression, made up her mind to write to York at once. The only question was whether it were best to write to Mrs. Rockingham or Ellen. She was quite aware that she did not quite hit it off with her niece, but then she was quite alive to her being a very much stronger character than her mother. Still, Aunt Mary could not help thinking that Ellen would be very much shocked at the calling it had pleased her brother to adopt. It might be lucrative; he might be a great success in it; but surely it was rather *infra dig.* for a Rockingham to be riding racehorses for hire.

She knew that, though Ellen was no doubt sincere in her Calvinistic doctrines, humility entered but smally into her profession of faith. She judged rightly, that her niece would carry her head high as ever in adversity, being quite aware that Ellen was as proud a girl as ever stepped. She felt pretty sure that Mrs. Rockingham and her daughter must be still in ignorance of this caprice—so Aunt Mary called it to herself—of Gerald's. Still, it was only right that they should be made acquainted with it, now poor Alister was gone. Gerald had nobody to look to for advice but his mother and aunt, and a boy of eighteen required some guidance in shaping his life.

Ah! Aunt Mary, you don't know that boys with any grit in them settle these things best for themselves, and without much reference to their womankind.

So Aunt Mary sat down and indited a letter to her niece, in which she told the story of Gerald's career as far as she had been able to learn it. There were plenty of people who were able to narrate the history of Jim Forrest, but Miss Stacey was a little shy in her inquiries if she thought people the least aware that she was that rising horseman's aunt. Still, so much was it the topic of conversation, that in a few days she had got over all sensitiveness on that point. The men—and their opinion does count for something in the long run—were pretty well unanimous in their admiration both of his pluck and his horsemanship.

"When a fellow's ruined, by Jove! you know, what's a fellow to do?" observed the Hon. Bob Maxley, who, having reached that same crisis some ten years previously, had lived comfortably on his friends and relations ever since. "He's quite right to see if he can't get back some of the money the confounded beggars took from his father"—a speech which, though a little incoherent, insomuch as that the bookmakers, who follow the *figures*, should in the long run invariably get the best of the backers, who follow their *fancies*—simply meant that Alister Rockingham had shared the fate that has attended so many " all through a backing of the favourite!"

Even the women for the most part seemed to think there was nothing derogatory in the line Gerald had taken up. It was so eccentric!—it was so romantic! Then, he was a success! He was quite a lion, and they love that still more. Then, again, he was said to be good-looking, and tongues were wagging much about him; and, finally, when Lady Di Franton declared she would bring up her youngest boy to the same profession, Aunt Mary altogether succumbed before the verdict of that sporting peeress, and wished now that she had unfolded the tale of Gerald's iniquity in less despondent fashion.

We are all influenced more or less by the opinions of our fellows—women more especially—and with good reason, for none of them can afford to ignore any combined opinion of their own sex. Aunt

Mary suddenly found herself quite a person of some little importance, simply owing to her relationship with the fashionable jockey. That all this should produce a complete reaction in Aunt Mary's opinion was only natural. Upon first hearing of Gerald's career she had felt not a little ashamed; now, as might have been expected, she waxed rather garrulous concerning it, and pronounced his conduct noble; nay, heroic! confided to her hearers that her nephew was the grandest horseman this or any other age had seen, and then proceeded to recount sundry of his youthful exploits on his pony with the York and Ainsty, or over the Cranley pastures.

At length Aunt Mary received a reply to her letter. Ellen's answer ran as follows:—

"My dear Aunt,—

"You know how anxious we have been

about Gerald and what he was doing, but even that anxiety was easier to bear than the dreadful tidings you sent us. How he can so utterly have forgoten what he owes to his family as to accept such employment as you talk of would be beyond my comprehension but for one thing. He is the victim at present of an unfortunate entanglement with a young person, the daughter of a man of that class; and though, in the first instance, I looked upon it as a mere boyish flirtation, I fear it is likely to end much more seriously.

"I fancy I can hear you say, 'You don't mean he is thinking of marrying her?' Yes, my dear aunt; I am very much afraid that is what he will do, in spite of all our remonstrances. You don't know how Gerald has altered of late. He has become so hard and obstinate, and takes his own way about things without reference to mamma or me. That the strange career he has adopted was at this young woman's suggestion I have no doubt; that our united persuasions will fail to induce him to abandon it I have also no doubt, and yet surely it is our duty to try what we can do.

"Here Gerald's dreadful secret is as yet unknown, but for you, Aunt Mary, how I pity you! I wonder how you ever dare face society. It must be so very awkward to be stared at as the near relative of a professional jockey, or to have to listen to the comments made on Gerald's conduct by those ignorant of the relationship. Our ruin, except for mamma's sake, I felt but little, and cannot help saying that I think Gerald might have spared us this disgrace. I will send you his address as soon as I know it, and you will write to him, won't you? It is our duty to do all we can to save him from the life of degradation he has chosen.

"Good bye. Kindest love from mamma, who, like myself, is quite upset by this new affliction.

"Ever, dear Aunt Mary,

"Your affectionate niece,

"Ellen Rockingham."

The news that Gerald meant to marry among those of his vocation was a blow Miss Stacey was quite unprepared for. She knew very well that though society in its caprice might applaud "Jim Forrest," the successful jockey, and even make a lion of him, they would not recognise his wife if she sprang from that class; and then Aunt Mary pictured a buxom young woman with hoydenish manner as unlike Dollie as possible, and knit her brows as she wondered what the family would be able to make of her. However, she reflected Gerald was only just nineteen, and Ellen probably overrated his obstinacy. When he was seriously talked to by them all, he would no doubt see that this could not be. Boys did get engaged in this ridiculous fashion sometimes but nothing ever came of it. Gerald's offending would terminate, no doubt, in the usual fashion.

CHAPTER II.

ELLEN CONSULTS JOHN THORNDYKE.

HER letter to Aunt Mary barely conveyed Ellen's real view on the subject of Gerald's offending. She really could not have been more horrified at hearing her brother was somebody's stud-groom; a most respectable and trustworthy position, no doubt, but not one that any girl, born a lady, could feel anything but shocked at finding her brother holding. She racked her brain as to what was to be done. That anything she, her mother, or her aunt could say would turn him from his course she utterly disbelieved, but that he was to be left to continue such a disgraceful calling without stern remonstrances on the part of his near relatives Ellen thought would be monstrous, and argue disgraceful neglect of a mere boy on their part. But who was to speak to him? Ah, that was not quite so easy to say. There were plenty of people, no doubt, who might speak, but to whom of them was Gerald likely to pay the slightest attention? To those related or connected with him, Miss Rockingham made answer to herself—None.

Then Ellen had an inspiration—what if she should ask John Thorndyke to expostulate with him? She did not herself at all hold with those very Broad Church views which characterised the Rector of St. Margaret's, but her common sense told her that, could they be brought together, this was the man of all others to talk to about her brother and the disgrace he was bringing upon his family. And yet she felt a little shy about entering into family affairs with Mr. Thorndyke. Still, who was she to speak to? Something must be done, and at once, and, if anyone could appeal to Gerald with some chance of success, the liberal-minded and whilom sporting Rector—for he owned freely and mirthfully to that backsliding—was, she thought, the man to do it. Miss Rockingham had seen a good deal of John Thorndyke lately, and had conceived a great respect and esteem for him. She still held that his bold views and frank outspoken treatment of things religious savoured of want of reverence, yet she was fain to confess that she could not call Mr. Thorndyke himself irreverent, while she acknowledged that the man was thoroughly honest and in earnest. If his treatment of his parishioners was, to say the best of it, peculiar in her eyes, she knew that he nevertheless worked hard amongst them, and had undoubtedly won their confidence and regard, while those short stirring addresses, with a good deal of sting in them, too, at times, she saw, roused the congregation in a manner that she looked in vain for elsewhere. Miss Rockingham wondered at times whether Mr. Thorndyke might not understand how to influence men's hearts better than Mr. Brushley, who, though he preached at considerable length, was wont to have a soporific effect among his hearers. She was still a constant attendant in the latter's church, and took no inconsiderable part in the work of that parish, but in this, her hour of trouble, it was John Thorndyke whose help she determined to seek, and not that of the clergyman of her election. Ellen felt instinctively that Gerald would listen with scant patience to an appeal from Mr. Brushley, but thought somehow with John Thorndyke it might be different.

It was a cold, raw November day that Ellen, wrapped in furs, relics of her former grandeur, of the time when she was Miss Rockingham of Cranley Chase, made her way across the city in the direction of Walmgate Bar.

The parish of St. Margaret's clustered round the splendid old gate, which, with barbican and portcullis, dominates the Hull Road, standing in rather a poor-looking part of the city, tenanted in great measure by the artisan class. Ellen had never been to Mr. Thorndyke's house before, but had no difficulty in finding it, there being plenty of people ready to point out where t'parson lived. In answer to her inquiry Miss Rockingham was informed that Mr. Thorndyde was out, but would probably be in before many minutes. Would she step in and wait?

"I'll show you into the study, if you'll excuse it, Miss," said the servant girl in response to Ellen's assent. "There is no fire in the drawing-room, and it's a raw morning. Master said he should be in by this, and he's mostly pretty close to his time."

Ellen looked round the room with the curiosity we all feel upon first seeing the sanctum of any one in whom we feel interested. It was not a large room by any means, and the walls were lined from top to bottom with bookcases. In the centre stood a writing-table, not a gimcrack dandified davenport, but a large, serviceable oaken one, covered with dark leather, and well garnished with drawers. Another plain, square table in the window, a comfortable armchair on either side of the fireplace, and a few other chairs scattered about, pretty well completed the furniture of the apartment. The tops of the bookcases were decorated with the busts of some of the most illustrious Greek and English poets — Æschylus and Homer, Shakespeare and Milton, &c., while the bookcases contained a *mélange* that would have misled any one studying their contents considerably as to the position in the world occupied by their proprietor. Rows of the Greek dramatists and of the English classics clothed the shelves on the one side of the room, while on the other was a nearly complete edition of the "Racing Calendar," works on farming, treatises on angling, beginning with Izaak Walton, and then going down to what the more modern writers on scientific fishing had written on the subject. Judging from that room you would have pronounced the master of the house a scholar and a sportsman, but there was nothing suggestive that he was a clergyman.

Ellen had not to wait long before Mr. Thorndyke entered.

"Charmed to see you, Miss Rockingham, though I regret that I should have kept you waiting. Still I am glad that my people had the *nous* to show you into a room where there was a fire."

"I have come to consult you about a

rather painful business," said Ellen, as she shook hands.

"I am sorry to hear it," replied Thorndyke, "but don't be in a hurry. Take your own time to tell me what your trouble is. I need scarcely say you are welcome to any advice or assistance I can give. Nothing the matter with Mrs. Rockingham, I trust?"

"No, thank you, my mother is quite well. It is about my brother that I wish to speak to you."

John Thorndyke made no reply, but quietly dropped into the armchair opposite Ellen, and waited for her to begin. He knew at once that she had at last discovered how Gerald was earning his bread, and from what the rector knew of Miss Rockingham's feelings on such points guessed that the discovery was a cruel mortification to her.

"You know how anxious we were to find out where my brother was and what he was doing; we have heard at last, and, oh, Mr. Thorndyke, it's too dreadful—too disgraceful. He is getting his living as a common jockey!"

"Not quite that, Miss Rockingham, for he is already eminent in the profession of his adoption. You must forgive me neither feeling surprised nor shocked at what you tell me. I have known it some time. I don't know why, but last August, at Durnford's, when Farrington told us the history of Jim Forrest, I jumped at the conclusion that he was your brother. Still it was not till a couple of months later that I found my surmise was correct, and the confirmation of it came in a letter Farrington wrote to Durnford, in which he said, 'Fancy, my gentleman jockey, the Jim Forrest I told you about, turns out to be the brother of that handsome Miss Rockingham whom I met at your house last summer.'"

"Yes; my aunt wrote word that the

story was in every one's mouth. Poor Aunt Mary! No doubt, she hardly dare go out for fear of being pointed at as the lady who has got a professional jockey for a nephew."

"Quite the reverse, I imagine, from what I hear. There is something so romantic in the idea of a son recovering from the quicksands of the turf the argosy his father lost therein that your brother, Miss Rockingham, if he chose, might be the lion of the day. Titled and fashionable ladies would compete for his company at their table; but I am told he lives the life of an anchorite, and is not to be wooed from his seclusion by mere 'cakes and ale' or 'ginger hot i' the mouth.'"

"Mr. Thorndyke!" cried Ellen, rising indignantly, "I come to you in my trouble, and you jeer at me — make a jest of what assuredly is no jesting matter to me."

"Miss Rockingham," said the rector

quietly, but with a sternness the girl had never encountered before in his manner, "I am not in the habit of jeering at people who come to me in their hour of sorrow. My office brings before me too many tales of real suffering that I am powerless to alleviate not to leave me tender-hearted and, I trust, sympathetic. If I have treated your trouble somewhat lightly, it is because it is imaginary. I have told you what I firmly believe to be the truth concerning it. Your brother is not held by the world to have disgraced himself, but, on the contrary, to have distinguished himself, and might, if he chose, be the lion of the hour."

"You can't really mean this, Mr. Thorndyke!" cried Ellen, perfectly aghast at such an utterly new reading of Gerald's conduct.

"Indeed I do. I look upon it that the world generally have the good sense to recognise the pluck and independent spirit that led your brother to turn to and support himself in the manner he best might, instead of sponging on his friends for the miserable bread of indolence. Remember, Miss Rockingham, that it is not given to all of us to follow the path in life we would have fain chosen for ourselves."

"And I counted upon you to speak to him, and point out the disgrace he was bringing upon his name and family," murmured Ellen.

"But I don't see that he is doing anything of the kind," rejoined Thorndyke. "Although I have no plea on which to intrude my advice upon your brother, still, had he fallen into vicious courses, or amongst evil associates, I would have done your bidding, Miss Rockingham. Gerald is leading a healthful life, and following a profession that requires energy, abstinence, and self-control. A young fellow can go through no better discipline; the worst of it is it's a little too severe, and apt to produce a reaction resulting in a very Capua of self-indulgence."

"And you don't think we ought to remonstrate with him?" exclaimed Ellen, in a state of unmitigated surprise at the view Mr. Thorndyke took of her brother's proceedings.

"I think you had better leave Gerald to himself. From the independence of character he has already shown I should say he has taken his future into his own hands, and is little likely to brook remonstrance or advice from any one."

"I don't know what to think about it," replied Ellen, sadly.

"Miss Rockingham, let me tell you a little story," said the Rector, quietly. "When I was at the University there was a young fellow there from whom great things were expected in the future. He was not only amongst the foremost in the cricket-field, and devoted to all kinds of sport, but he stood high in the estimation of the dons besides, for he worked, as he played, with all his might, and fought his way upwards till he was not only in the University Eleven, but had taken high honours to boot. The Bar was the career he had marked out for himself, and he was about to leave the University and commence the pursuit of fortune in that arduous profession, when the sudden death of his father changed the whole current of his life. His father was a quiet country clergyman, who died, leaving behind him a shy, delicate widow and an invalid daughter, besides this young fellow at college. The mother, as those shy, sensitive women always do, trembled at the bare idea of transplantation, whilst the daughter was equally dismayed at the idea of facing a new world. Where they were they knew every one; they had numerous friends even amongst the tradespeople. The late rector had been very popular, and at the earnest request of the parishioners, backed by the strong testimonials in his favour of the authorities of his college, the bishop offered the living to his son, proposing to put in a curate in charge till such time as the son could get ordained, and otherwise qualify. Whether he did rightly or no is not for me to say, but my friend, after taking one night to think over it, accepted the bishop's offer. It was the one way he could keep a comfortable home, much less the home they were attached to, over the heads of his mother and sister. You may say he had no right to embrace so sacred a vocation without feeling a decided call for it. He acted as he thought right. He sacrificed himself for those nearest and dearest to him, and, from the moment he elected to take up the cross, abandoned all those pursuits of which hitherto he had been so passionately fond, as incompatible with his new profession. Like your brother, Miss Rockingham, he was compelled to embark in a career not of his own electing, but whatsoever his hand found to do he did it with all his might, and has ever laboured honestly and conscientiously to do his duty in that path of life to which it pleased God—not himself, mind—to call him. A man, I hold, can do no more."

John Thorndyke became silent, and was apparently absorbed in reverie. Ellen broke the stillness by never a word.

At last she spoke.

"Mr. Thorndyke, you are wiser and better than I; and I beg your pardon for troubling you with my foolish pride. Your story—for of course it is your own—is strangely like my brother's; but—but you had the alternative of—I can't help saying it—embracing the profession of a gentleman; while poor Gerald——"

"Had to embrace a more healthy, lucrative, and, to him, congenial career.

Pray, don't distress yourself about your brother, Miss Rockingham. You will find most men and women, whose opinion is worth having, ay, and worldly people, too, will endorse my opinion, and admire your brother's pluck and independence."

"I hope we may get used to it in time," replied Ellen, with just a slight shake in her voice; for this really was a serious trouble to the girl; "and that Aunt Mary may not find it a serious annoyance in society. And now I must say good-bye, with many apologies for trespassing so long upon your good nature. Only one question more," she added softly. "I trust your mother and sister are happy?"

"They have both been at rest now some years, Miss Rockingham; but that their last days on earth were tranquil was an inexpressible consolation to me. Good-bye."

John Thorndyke escorted her to the door bareheaded; and, as Ellen walked home, she thought about the Rector of St. Margaret's in a way she never had yet. He had become a hero in her eyes.

CHAPTER III.

THE DANCING MASTER PROVES INCORRIGIBLE.

A LETTER from Aunt Mary confirmatory of Thorndyke's words did much to reconcile Ellen to Gerald's present course of life. That it was right for a Rockingham to ride races for hire she could not believe, any more than it would be that he should drive a cab. It was a comfort to find that the world looked leniently upon it, and regarded the affair apparently as a piece of pardonable eccentricity. She was not blind to the independent spirit Gerald had shown, and upon what John Thorndyke had laid such stress, but she did wish it had taken some other direction. Surely he might have found something better to do than race-riding. Ellen did not know what a well-paid profession jockeyship was in these days, nor did she quite understand the difficulty a young gentleman, with no special qualifications, had about finding something to do.

Suddenly it occurred to Ellen that she had forgotten to confide to Mr. Thorndyke the more serious part of Gerald's offending—to wit, his contemplated marriage. Surely Mr. Thorndyke would not approve of Gerald's marrying out of his class. That could have nothing to do with "the spirit of independence" so much lauded, and even the Rector of St. Margaret's, liberal as he was in his ideas, could hardly approve of such a fusion of classes as that marriage would be. Then it suddenly occurred to Miss Rockingham that, much as she valued the opinion of John Thorndyke, it was quite possible her brother might see no necessity for the rector's approval on a matter so nearly concerning himself. Moreover, Mr. Thorndyke had already declared that he had no plea upon which to interfere in Gerald's affairs, and given her to understand that only to rescue the lad from a dissolute life, and at the earnest desire of his people, could he have any pretext for meddling with Gerald in any way. Now Gerald was doing nothing of that sort, but was leading a steady, hard-working life from all accounts, so Ellen sorrowfully came to the conclusion that it would be useless to ask his advice about that siren Dollie.

The dead season, as racing men call it, had now commenced; that is to say, the legitimate racing year was finished, and till the saddling-bell pealed forth on the Carholme at Lincoln turfites had nothing to do but to study the "Calendar" and discuss the events of the past twelve months. No story perhaps more bandied about than that of Gerald Rockingham, for all race-goers, as well as society, knew now that he and Jim Forrest were one. Gerald had thrown off all disguise about it, and, though he still retained his assumed name of "Jim Forrest," frankly admitted to all who cared to know that he was the son of Alister Rockingham.

The promulgation of his real name, to tell the truth, promised to do the young fellow considerable good. He had already shown that he was an artist in the saddle, capable of holding his own with the foremost jockeys of the day, and many an old friend of his father's followed Lord Whitby's example, and promised to give him a turn when the game began again.

Gerald, of course, wrote openly now to his own people concerning his career. He told them how well he was doing, how he had already money in the bank, and how high were his hopes for the future. About Dollie he said nothing, but Ellen did not augur there was any likelihood of his engagement falling through from such ominous silence. Still, all that winter, though his letters were frequent, he never came to York. He remitted more than one comfortable little cheque to St. Leonard's Place, but pleaded he was too busy studying his profession to have time even to run up at Christmas, at which Mrs. Rockingham made vehement protest. But it was no use, Gerald remained resolutely at Newmarket, where he volunteered to give a canter, when weather permitted, to any horse requiring one, and Mr. Pipes, with whom he had become a great favourite, more than once invited him to give some of the Panton Lodge colts "a lesson," which his patience, tact, and delicacy of hand made really invaluable to a nervous young one. But this Gerald steadily declined to do. He made some trivial excuse at first, but at last told the trainer right out that, handsomely as Sir Marmaduke had always behaved to him, he could not forget that the baronet had taken his jacket away, and, therefore, he could not think of interfering in his stable without express orders from him, which, as Sir Marmaduke was away gambling at Nice, shooting pigeons, and fruitlessly endeavouring to break the bank at Monte Carlo, he could hardly be expected to give.

Still, Gerald worked hard that winter, and was constantly on the back of some awkward-tempered colt, employed in the not very enviable task of teaching it manners, and before the public were hurrying to Lincoln to once more try to pick the winner of that most difficult of handicaps, and lose their money by backing the always beaten favourite for "the Brocklesby's," the Newmarket trainers had come to the conclusion that there wasn't a lad at Newmarket that could communicate such confidence to a nervous "young one" as Jim Forrest, and many were the good-natured assurances that he needn't fear but what he'd get plenty of riding in the coming season.

We have all our days, our seasons! What ordinary shooting man does not remember the day on which it seemed he couldn't go wrong, could not miss them if he tried? Many of us can recall that day in the racket-court when we played a good seven aces over our game, and astonished our friends in the gallery not a little. Billiards the same; and what hunting-man does not recollect the time he got well away with the leading hounds, slipping the whole field by a quarter of a mile or so, and, his blood up, rode as he never did before or since? So it is with racing, and old turfites can recollect "Sir Joseph's," year, more than one of them: but '51 will do for a sample, Mr. Merry's, "The Baron's," a very constellation of triumphs, and latterly, Lord Falmouth's. This coming season was destined to be known in turf-lore as Lord Whitby's and Jim Forrest's year. The fates, tired at last, it may be presumed, of persecuting that irascible nobleman, seemed to have handed him over to be the spoilt child of Fortune; and from the Craven Meeting all through the year his lordship's well-known colours were seen continually in the van. True to his word, he had commenced by giving Jim Forrest some of his riding, and Jim was not the man to throw away a chance when he really had a good horse under him. As he scored victory after victory for his employer, Lord Whitby, to whom a series of successes were extremely titillating on account of the rarity with which such triumphs had been vouchsafed him, was in high good humour with his new jockey. He somewhat over-estimated his horsemanship, and, forgetting that he had a better lot of colts than it had ever been his luck to own before, vowed that Jim

Forrest was the best jockey on the turf; "and then, by Jove, sir, he's a Rockingham, and one knows he'll ride straight," a remark which, though doubtless true of Gerald, conveyed a rather unfair insinuation against the majority of his colleagues.

Sir Marmaduke, on the contrary, and his followers, had so far been singularly unfortunate. Mr. Pipes had the mischance to get that bane of trainers, influenza, into his stable, with the usual result —his charges all the first part of the season were rarely quite themselves, while in some of the worst cases it had been found hopeless to get them ready, and more than one rich stake, which had been apparently at Sir Marmaduke's mercy, had to be abandoned, because his representative was *hors de combat*. Notable the case this with the flying Atalanta, who had proved herself about the best two-year-old in training last season. She was very heavily engaged, and apparently her taking the One Thousand Guineas and Oaks was a mere question of health. She had been smitten so badly with this curse of racing stables that it was questionable whether she would ever recover her form during the present campaign, and what made the matter still worse was the well-known fact that when fillies, in racing parlance, lose their form at three years old, they are apt to never recover it.

Even in this Jim Forrest's star was to a certain extent in the ascendant, for Sir Marmaduke, upon hearing from Mr. Pipes what Forrest had said when asked to handle some of his horses in the winter, chose to take umbrage at Jim's refusal, and consequently never offered him a mount, whereby Jim was probably spared discomforture on more than one occasion, as the baronet's string apparently couldn't win even a selling race.

You may be sure Jim's career was

closely watched in St. Leonard's Place.
The widow took to studying the sporting-
news again as she had been used to at the
zenith of her husband's turf career, but
with infinitely less trepidation than had
come to her in latter days. She did not
associate, poor soul, any danger with the
race-course, except that of gambling, and
she was assured that Gerald did not do
that; nor did he. He bet at times, as
everybody connected with the turf does,
but he could not be called a regular
speculator. Still, he was putting together
a very nice little nest-egg, and towards
this Lord Whitby, who was as open-
handed as he was hot-tempered, not a
little contributed. He was now most
thoroughly established in the very front
rank of his profession, in receipt of re-
taining salaries from both Lord Whitby
and another well-known magnate of the
sporting world. Sir Marmaduke more
than once regretted his severance with

Jim Forrest; "not but what," he would say ruefully to his great ally, Captain Farrington, "it don't much matter who's up on such a lot of half-trained devils as all ours are this season." There was one exception, and that was the Dancing Master; the influenza had affected him but slightly, and merely necessitated a slight stoppage in his work during that bitter spring time. Mr. Pipes, like Bill Greyson, had conceived an immense opinion of the horse's capabilities; but he also recognised that the horse equally had an opinion about when it was necessary to exert himself, and that unfortunately seldom coincided with that of his owner and trainer. Mr. Pipes was used to deal with all sorts of equine temper; but he candidly confessed that "the Dancer" was a puzzler.

He tried—as all trainers do nowadays who know their business — coaxing, patience, and the tenderest handling;

but "the Dancer" was not to be cajoled with lumps of sugar, either practically or metaphorically. That wilful quadruped had sucked in the idea apparently with his mother's milk—she *was* a jaundiced-tempered matron—that he was to have his own way in this weary world, and could not be got to comprehend that horses are born to servitude. No; they could make nothing of him in the Panton Lodge stable. When he was tried just before the Claret Stakes, at the Craven Meeting, he galloped like a lion, and in the *argot* of the racecourse made his antagonists lie down; but in the actual race, three days afterwards, he never showed at all, and Blackton once more energetically pronounced him the greatest coward in training.

"It's not that, Sir Marmaduke," replied Mr. Pipes in answer to Blackton's remark just after the race, "the beggar can stay, and is game enough when he means winning, but, damme, I can't help thinking he stands in with the bookmakers, and runs for them instead of for us whenever he's backed."

"I don't quite know what to think, Pipes. He failed at Epsom, the same at Doncaster, and now again, over the 'Ditch In' for the Clarets. He wins over the Rowley Mile, the only time he ever wins. It looks to me as if he couldn't get further, and that he's been run ever since out of his distance."

"It's not that, Sir Marmaduke," replied the trainer, "it's his beastly temper."

"It's his want of heart," said Blackton, as he turned and walked sulkily away.

"Get him ready for the Hunt Cup at Ascot," said the baronet, curtly. "If he gets in well—and he must—I'll stand him a raker for that, and if he fails us then Bill Greyson may have him back again at once. Better he paid for his corn than me."

In writing the wonderfully romantic narrative of Gerald Rockingham's unprecedented turf career, it is difficult to keep clear of the mistake of becoming a mere volume of the Racing Calendar. Continuous repetition of sporting stories of the same description is apt to wax tedious; indeed, in these times it is so easy to bear a little too heavily upon any subject, and, writing as I do within half a mile of Westminster, I may surely add, talk too much on any subject. Parliament Street is thick with verbiage, national business is at a standstill, while the six hundred and fifty windbags that represent the nation are still busily engaged in emulous cackle.

For the above reason it is necessary to pass somewhat rapidly over the racing of this year, and simply record the fact that the Dancing Master was allotted a weight in the Hunt Cup which, conjoined with the fact that the horse was extremely well, made the Panton Lodge people regard his chance as an immense one, should he only take it into his head to run kindly. Sir Marmaduke adhered to his before-expressed intention, and backed the horse to win him an enormous stake, which he was easily enabled to do, from the known uncertainty of the animal's temper, at a very liberal price. Once more did the erratic Dancing Master betray the confidence of his new owner. Indulging in quite uncalled-for gambols at the post, he got a very indifferent start when the flag eventually fell, but, going like a bolt from a catapult when he did go, his tremendous speed enabled him to catch his horses as the hill was topped, and the gay-coloured troop came within view of the stand. Anxious to take a good place, Blackton immediately afterwards hustled him a little, and just as Farrington exclaimed, "he means it at last, Marm," the uncertain brute determined not to be put out of his way by any one, shut up, and declined to make another effort.

This last exhibition of the grey's temper was enough for the baronet; he came to the conclusion that Blackton was right, and that the colt was a rank coward, and ordered his trainer to send him back to Riddleton forthwith. To Mr. Pipes's suggestion that they had better keep the colt a little longer, Sir Marmaduke replied curtly,

"Certainly not; I can't afford to give him another chance. He's cost me about twenty thousand already, first and last, and would be a perpetual temptation if I kept him on the premises. Send him back to Greyson next week. He may be the best colt in the kingdom, but he'd break the Bank of England."

CHAPTER IV.

GERALD VISITS YORK.

IF his own people had not seen Gerald, neither had his sweetheart. Since that hurried visit just after Egham Meeting he had not set foot in Yorkshire; he had intended then to have returned in a week and take part in the various contests on the Knavesmire, but, as we have seen, false pride had caused him not to keep that engagement. Dollie hardly knew what to think of things. It was true that Gerald wrote lovingly and frequently, and spoke in the most sanguine way of the future; but the girl did think that if he cared about her as much as he pretended, he would have found time during all those winter months to run up and see her. She knew very well that he had openly avowed his name, and that all the world were now aware who Jim Forrest really was, and she had been not a little amused at the way her father and mother had taken the information.

"Dal it all!" exclaimed Bill Greyson when he heard it; "to think that I've had a son of the squire's in my stable. I'm main sorry to think it. And that he should win the Two Thousand for Riddleton a few months after Riddleton had broke his father. It's like a dream. We ought all to be ashamed of ourselves that we didn't tell the squire about Phaeton."

As for Mrs. Greyson, she completely changed her note, declared that she had always noticed something very superior about Forrest's manner; rallied Dollie about her flirtation; and would simper and say, "I daresay the young squire will give us a look in before long. We know of an attraction at Riddleton that's likely to bring him north, don't we, Dollie?"

"Don't put such rubbish into a girl's head," the trainer would roughly interpose on such occasions. "He may have taken up race-riding for a season, but men of Gerald Rockingham's blood don't mate with such as us."

And then Dollie would toss her head disdainfully as woman does when it is suggested the victim may break the toils; they never believe it, and draw the gyves tighter and tighter, despite the warning of worldly-wise sisters, until one day the fetters lie riven, and the captive is gone, never to be re-captured.

But as the months rolled by, and Gerald never appeared either at York or Riddleton, Dollie began to feel not a little uncomfortable. If this had been mere flirtation, incense gratifying to her girlish vanity, it would have been cause of doubt and dismay that her lover could stay away so long from her; but it was much more than that. Dollie knew, alas! that she had given her whole heart to Gerald Rockingham, and, if he deemed that a bauble not worth keeping, God help her! for she would need it sorely. Could her father be right? Could Miss Rockingham be right? Was Gerald only amusing himself, as she had read and heard young men were wont to with women, more especially when they did not belong to their own station in life? and then Dollie would throw herself into the arm-chair near her casement, and, as she gazed across the broad undulating grassy expanse, the tears would well up into her eyes, and she would wonder whether the world really was so hollow and heartless as all that came to.

That "the world is hollow and their

doll stuffed with sawdust" is a phrase that most young women go through in their early days.

Gerald had conceived a great idea, and was working up to it with all the steady persistency that misfortune had called forth in his character. He had heard from Writson that all chance of disposing of Cranley in the aggregate seemed hopeless, and that he should be compelled to lot it and dispose of it piecemeal. Now Gerald, thanks to the liberal presents he had received, in the first instance from Sir Marmaduke and his followers, and latterly from Lord Whitby, had no less than between two and three thousand pounds at his banker's. He worked hard and lived sparingly, and, except the money he sent to assist the *ménage* at St. Leonard's Place, spent little of his earnings. He was now making a very good income, and the idea had come to him to embark the bulk of his savings in some turf speculation; to go for one great *coup*, and, should that come off, with the proceeds to purchase Cranley; not the manor, of course, but simply the house and chase. The difficulty was, what should the plotted *coup* consist of? He had ridden several colts of Lord Whitby's this year, whose winning might be regarded as fairly certain; but then the prices laid against these at starting had been so short, that it required to risk much more than he could afford to win the stake he wanted.

Gerald had for months been puzzling as to how the solution of his puzzle could be come by, but see it he couldn't, and meanwhile he heard from Writson that the handbills would be out early in August, and the sale take place about the beginning of September. Gerald reflected sadly that there remained but a very short time to plan and execute the stroke he meditated. Stockbridge and the Newmarket July Meetings were gone and past, and though Goodwood loomed before him he could see nothing in the programme that seemed suitable to his purpose. Suddenly it struck Jim that he would take a few days' holiday, run up to York, and see his mother and sister and Dollie.

It was with a big jump of the heart that Dollie received the letter in which Gerald announced his intention of coming northwards. Ah, this would clear up all doubts! Let her but see Gerald, and she would speedily be assured as to whether he loved her still; but she did not want to see him at Riddleton, and that was where she was when she received his letter. She looked forward to the rather slavish adulation that she felt sure her mother would accord "Mr. Rockingham" with as much dismay as the blunt mistrust of her father. So Dollie made up her mind that she must abandon the sweet summer moorland breezes for the hot, dusty city of York, and once more take up her abode with Uncle Thomas in Coney Street.

Mrs. Greyson was not disposed to wrangle with her daughter according to her wont. Had not that young woman captured what, in the good lady's estimation, was a stag royal, and, although she knew enough of the science of deer-stalking to comprehend that—

> Let the stricken deer go weep

did not at all mean that he was "gathered," that these sorely wounded ones often struggled on to the next forest and then took to themselves another mate, yet Mrs. Greyson, with half-closed eyes, kept on purring to herself over Dollie's approaching marriage with the heir of Cranley Chase. It mattered nothing that she knew, as all Yorkshire knew, that Cranley Chase was for sale, and Gerald a ruined a man riding races for a living. In her extreme satisfaction at her daughter marrying a man of gentle blood she ignored the sad story of the past few years, and chose to regard Gerald as holding the position his father had occupied when she first knew him.

Bill Greyson, on the contrary, took a very different view of his daughter's engagement. He admired Jim Forrest much; he recognised his great qualities as a horseman, and had heard from many of his Newmarket compatriots how steady he was in his life, and how steadfast in the pursuit of his new profession. As a brilliant jockey and a straightgoing young fellow the old trainer would have held Jim Forrest a most eligible suitor for his daughter's hand, but, when it turned out that Jim Forrest was Gerald Rockingham, it was different. A wild, hot-blooded lot the Rockinghams!—ever reckless in their passions as regarded wine, women, or play: such was their reputation on the country side; and the late Squire had shown himself impregnated with the old Adam in his youth to the full as much as his ancestors. Gréyson could hardly believe that, ruined or not ruined, Gerald Rockingham could mean to act fairly by his daughter. To a man of his birth the most obvious solution of his difficulties was a wealthy marriage. Groping dimly in the dark, the trainer had sense in his reasoning. In the state of transition in which we are all now living the money-grubbers, in their anxiety to turn butterflies, are only too keen to barter wealth for position, though how long we shall be before diamonds, a brown-fronted stone house, a silver-gilt dinner-service, and a pair of thousand-guinea carriage horses, constitute the *summum bonum* of existence, after the manner of our New York cousins, is a matter of conjecture. Birth and family are likely to count for much, while the dollar will be all-powerful in the days that lie before us.

Greyson honestly wanted to see no more of Jim Forrest save on a racecourse. He liked him in every respect except as a suitor for his daughter, though he still felt a little uncomfortable that Alister Rockingham's son should ever have been a stable-boy of his. A life past in the chicanery of the turf, and Bill Greyson (to put it mildly) had been at all events mixed up with some ugly turf stories in his time, had not altogether blunted the veteran's ideas of right. Although he had honestly done him a good turn, he still harped upon the fact that the son of his old freehanded employer, Alister Rockingham, should have been employed by him in a menial capacity. On the other hand, the thing he loved best on earth was Dollie, and his face hardened at the bare idea that a man should meditate wrong to her. It would be far safer, he thought, that the two should see no more of each other for the present. "As for the wife," he muttered to himself, "she's good in the dairy, and keeps a rare hand on 'em in the house, but she's a feather-pated woman, and no judge whatever of weights when it comes to match-making."

Dollie had, perhaps, exercised a wise discretion in not meeting her lover at Riddleton. The judicious pilot does not take his frail bark between Scylla and Charybdis unless necessity compels; those dangers are better avoided if possible, and the girl felt that neither of her parents was likely to be quite what she wished to Gerald at present. Besides she wanted to have him thoroughly to herself, and then she wondered whether she should see Miss Rockingham again, and whether Gerald meant to present her to his mother. She knew that he had announced his engagement to herself, but she had not come across Ellen since, and she was very anxious to meet that young lady under these altered circumstances.

If Dollie really entertained any doubts of her lover's constancy they were dispelled at once on Gerald's arrival at the drawing-room in Coney Street.

"Oh, Gerald!" she exclaimed, as she at length released herself from his passionate embrace, "what a time it is since I have seen you! Do you know how long it is, sir?"

"Yes, it is very nearly a year since I was last in York."

"And, if you are as fond of me as you pretend to be, how could you be so many months without coming near me?"

"Dangling at her apron-strings is not always the readiest way to win the girl you love. When there's man's work to be done, 'tis no time for such sweet fooleries. I only did your own bidding, Dollie, and now I am more successful than ever we hoped in the trade of your naming, surely you'd not have me give up 'silk,' and turn aside when I'm close to the top of the ladder."

"Of course not, Gerald. You know I wouldn't wish it for a moment, but you must expect a girl to pout a little at her lover's absence, even if she knows he is working hard for her sake. I don't suppose Rachel was very well satisfied with her father's arrangement, and, I have no doubt, felt quite as bad as Jacob did about it, when she found that she had, after all that waiting, to give way to her elder sister."

"Ah, well," said Gerald, laughing, "my servitude is not going to extend quite so long as that. I shall demand you of your parents before many months I trust. I have worked hard—aye, very hard!—and done better than I could have ever dreamt, and the end of it all is, darling, I have conceived a wilder dream than ever. I told you Cranley was in the market, and I am haunted with the idea of saving the house and park. Writson told me, and very sensibly, too, when last here, that it would be madness—that it would involve genteel pauperism—that most painful of all stages of poverty. "But," continued the lad, springing to his feet, and pacing the room in his excitement, "at that time I had very little money at the bank. I was by no means sure of making a good income by my profession. Now it is different. I am prepared to risk my small capital to effect a grand *coup*, and, should that be successful, I could save Cranley; while with the income I now make we could all live there if we were content to do so quietly, though comfortably."

"Oh, Gerald! that would be glorious! But what is to be the great stake that we are to play for?"

"Ah! that's just where it is, Dollie.

I don't know. I can't think of a *coup* to go for with what I call any reasonable chance of success."

"Stop, Gerald. Remember the horse that gave you your first great start—the horse that made you—the Dancing Master. Is'nt there something to be done with him?"

"There might be," said Gerald, meditatively; "but, you see, I never ride for Sir Marmaduke, now."

"But the horse is at Riddleton. They sent him back from Newmarket directly after Ascot. Sir Marmaduke, it seems, lost a lot of money over him in the Hunt Cup, and vowed he wasn't worth his keep. Father's got him back again."

"Well, it is possible there's a good race in him yet, if one could only catch him in the humour; but—even then I don't know when it's to be; and, Dollie, the time is so short. The Chase is to be sold in September."

"It's no use talking it over now," said the girl; "still, I've a presentiment that 'the Dancer' is our guardian angel, and he will take care of us yet. He doesn't mean to exert himself till you want him, Gerald; but don't forget he's at Riddleton, well, and—wicked old thing—anxious for a job. How long are we to keep you with us?"

"A couple of days or so is all I can spare. I have to see Writson, and I must call in St. Leonard's Place; but I have no end of engagements, and must get back south towards the end of the week."

"I was afraid it must be so. No, Gerald; I'm not repining, and I know that it is all for your good that you should be so fully occupied; but a young woman likes to keep a sweetheart she only sees once a year a little longer with her, if possible."

"Nonsense, Dollie; don't be unreasonable," exclaimed the young man, a little impatiently.

"I am not," replied the girl, softly. "I know it can't be; but I surely may regret that it is so."

Gerald's sole reply was of that description which is best left to the imagination. We can all recall what would have seemed appropriate under the circumstances, and human nature varies little with regard to these things.

"And now, Dollie," said young Rockingham, as the girl emerged from one of those unaccountable, but everyday, disappearances, which so troubled Bella Wilfer; "it's time I said good-bye. I've got to see Writson, and prepare my mother and sister to be introduced to you."

"Really, Gerald! Is Mrs. Rockingham anything like your sister? I shall feel so strange at meeting her."

"It would be much the same, whoever

I brought her, I think. She would never consider anyone quite good enough for her scapegrace son."

"I won't have you call yourself names," retorted Dollie, with a stamp of her pretty foot. " You know you are nothing of the kind. You never got into any row yet; and since—forgive me, Gerald, if I seem to speak hardly—you were left a beggar, you've honestly earned your own bread. Scapegrace, forsooth! I don't see much of that about you."

"Perhaps not," said Gerald, laughing, as he took up his hat; "but I must be off now; see Writson, and call in St. Leonard's Place. For the present, sweet, adieu."

"God bless and keep thee, dearest," rejoined Dollie, as she kissed him; and then Gerald went out into the soft summer air, and wended his way towards Mr. Writson's.

CHAPTER V.

A CALL ON ST. LEONARD'S PLACE.

GERALD's interview with Writson, although only what he expected, was nevertheless saddening. He had known for months that Cranley must go, but it was nevertheless a wrench to think that it was on the very verge now of passing away from the family. His principal object was to delay the sale, but he could not quite muster up courage to confide to the kind-hearted old lawyer the visionary hope he indulged in. It was all very well to tell his warm-hearted sanguine *fiancée* that he contemplated some daring turf speculation that would enable him to win money enough to redeem the Chase, but he felt it was a different thing to put this very undigested scheme before a hardheaded practical man. The scheme was as yet utterly immatured, and to get a business man to take into serious consideration that you meditate embarking in some gambling speculation to raise money is a thing not to be thought of. Mr. Writson, conscious that he had already delayed the sale to the utmost extent of his ability, not from the remotest idea of averting the blow, but simply from the hope that a purchaser might yet be found to take the estate in the lump, naturally failed to fathom Gerald's reason for further deferring it. There was no hope of assistance or rescue from any quarter. The lawyer felt like a surgeon who has conclusively made up his mind that an operation is imperative, and that it is childish on the part of the patient to wish to put it off any longer.

"I am sorry to say, Mr. Rockingham, that the creditors are not to be stayed further. I've exhausted the law's delay, and excuse me saying further postponement, even if possible, is unadvisable. Nobody can sympathise more sincerely with you under the circumstances than I do, but you must brace yourself up, sir, to meet the inevitable. A curious thing is that Pearson, I find, has been making inquiries about the Chase."

"Why, what can he want with it?" exclaimed Gerald. "After squeezing the orange all these years in conjunction with my precious cousin, he can't hanker after the rind."

"No, no, my dear sir," replied Writson, not a little astonished at Gerald's passionate outbreak. "It's not likely he wants it for himself, but he may have a commission to buy it. I shall very likely get at who it's for before the sale."

"By the way, has Mr. Elliston made

any further proposition with regard to those acceptances of his?"

"No; and, until we put the screw on him from a social point of view, I suspect it's very unlikely he will. He, through Pearson, as I wrote you word, offered a thousand pounds, but we ought to get double that out of him. The whole sum it's useless to expect. Now I see by the papers that you ride a great deal for Lord Whitby. On what sort of footing do you stand with him?"

"I'm a great favourite of his. I have been lucky with his horses, and, though he treats me always as if I stood on the same platform as himself, I never forget that at present I am his jockey, and it has done me no harm with him. He is, as you perhaps know, proud and passionate, but he was an old friend of my father's, and stretched out his hand to me on that account."

"It strikes me that he might be just

the man to put pressure on Mr. Elliston. If Lord Whitby chose to take up your case he is big enough to crush such as Mr. Elliston, and you owe it to Mrs. and Miss Rockingham to make him pay as much of his debt to your father as possible."

"I'll do it, Writson. I'll take the earliest opportunity of speaking to Lord Whitby on the subject. His dictum on all matters of honour is law in the racing world. Nobody ever ventures to question his decision."

"If that's so, I think it probable Mr. Elliston will come to terms sooner than have so awkward a story in circulation concerning him."

"We'll try it, at all events," said Gerald, rising. "There'll be little enough left for my mother and sister when all is done. There's nothing to warrant my not recovering that two thousand pounds, if I can. Cuthbert Elliston will be really our debtor for four thousand odd even then."

"Quite so," replied Mr. Writson. "Do you make any stay in York?"

"No. I must get back to-morrow or the next day at furthest. Good-bye."

The lawyer shook his head thoughtfully as Gerald left the room. "Ah!" he muttered, "it's very sad. A fine young fellow, and the best blood in Yorkshire, riding races for a living, and his heritage coming to the hammer in September."

Gerald's appearance in St. Leonard's Place was welcomed with a low cry of pleasure from Mrs. Rockingham; indeed, both ladies were unfeignedly glad to see him. They had quite got over their first dismay upon learning the career he had embraced, and discovered that the world generally saw nothing at all disgraceful in it. Then, was he not an only son and brother whom they had not seen for nearly a twelvemonth? It was small wonder they were disposed to make much of him.

"My dear boy, it's quite a treat to have you with us again," exclaimed Mrs. Rockingham. "Sit down and tell me who first put this extraordinary freak into your head. We are too thoroughly Yorkshire not to feel somewhat proud of your horsemanship. How on earth came you to think of it?"

"It was Dollie Greyson's idea; and without her help and encouragement I should never have carried it out. But, mother, dearest, to go back to first causes, Cuthbert Elliston made me take to the saddle. Surely you remember the cruel taunt he flung at me that day at Cranley when we learnt we were ruined. He recommended me to 'turn gamekeeper or pad-groom.' I had to do something, and, talking the matter over with Dollie, told her of Cuthbert's bitter gibe, and, her woman's wit suggested 'turn jockey.'

Curiously enough, the first race I won was on his horse. I won, and he had me turned out of the stable."

"What disgraceful ingratitude!" exclaimed Ellen. "I wonder all the racing world didn't cry shame upon him."

"Never expect gratitude from Cuthbert," rejoined Gerald, with a bitter smile. "Our poor father lent him thousands which he never repaid, except with undying hatred for all of us."

"I always did think he was your poor father's undoing," murmured Mrs. Rockingham, sadly.

"He hasn't quite settled with me yet," rejoined Gerald. "I fancy he's repented already of his sneering advice. My riding cost him a good deal at Goodwood last year."

"And you like the life, Gerald?—it interests you?" inquired Mrs. Rockingham.

"Yes, it's a healthy life, if hard; and

besides, I've done with the rough part of it. I had my turn of that in my novitiate at Riddleton. You know I was always fond of horses, and there's nothing more exciting than the final struggle for a big race, when you know that success depends principally upon your own nerve and judgment; that the calling on your horse for his supreme effort at the right moment means victory, while a couple of seconds too soon or too late is to lose the race."

"But your associates, Gerald; they must be so dreadful," said his sister.

"Some of them, of course, are pretty rough, but it's not necessary to see much of them, while others are very good fellows. They may not have quite the polish of society, but don't think they're uneducated. Many of the trainers, for instance, interest themselves in many things quite outside their profession."

Miss Rockingham had not quite got an answer to her insidious question. Since her brother had announced his firm intention of marrying Dollie Greyson, Ellen had become curious concerning Gerald's feminine acquaintance. Up to that time she had never given a passing thought to his marrying, but when a man, even though young, takes the idea of wanting a wife into his head, his sisters may naturally regard a sister-in-law as imminent. Ellen had hoped her question would draw forth some allusion to Dollie. She wanted much to hear whether Gerald had seen her constantly all these months. She knew his letters were always dated from the South, and that Dollie's home was in Yorkshire, but he might have been in Yorkshire many times, though he had never visited St. Leonard's Place, and whether he was as "infatuated about that chit of a trainer's daughter as ever" was a thing Miss Rockingham much desired to know.

"But," she said, returning to the

G 2

charge after a slight pause, "you used to be fond of ladies' society; surely you must miss that dreadfully in this life you have chosen?"

"A good many young fellows have to do without that at the outset of their career, and, though I fancy I am not quite the social pariah you picture me, still, I haven't time or inclination for that sort of thing. Remember, I have always this end before my eyes, I have adopted this profession as the pleasantest and easiest way in which I can make sufficient money to take my true position in the world, and further that I have probably but a short time to do it in. I'm not a light-weight now, and it's only by constant exercise and rigid abstinence that I keep about eight stone. It's quite likely that in a few years I shall get too heavy to ride. Besides," concluded Gerald, with a smile, "you forget my book's made."

"Surely, surely, you will never commit

such madness," said Ellen. "You are avowedly making money in an inferior position with which to resume your proper station as soon as possible. To marry Miss Greyson is to settle down in that class for life. Speak to him, mother—urge him, for all our sakes, to pause before he takes such an irrevocable step as that would be!"

"Indeed, my dear," said Mrs. Rockingham, "do think of what your sister says. It was a great trouble to us at first when we found out what you were doing, and it was only when Mr. Thorndyke explained to us that you were making a deal of money, and people in these times didn't care how that was done, providing it was only honestly, that we got reconciled to it, and began to understand what you have just told us. But Gerald, dearest, to marry amongst these people is to live and die amongst them."

"You can't understand," interposed

Gerald, roughly, "what Dollie's been to me. You can't suppose I'm going to throw over the girl I'm sincerely attached to, and to whose advice and assistance I owe my present position, because she's not in the Stud Book?"

"Your new associates begin to rather influence your conversation," rejoined Ellen, haughtily.

"Don't talk rubbish," said Gerald, sharply. "You might have heard my last remark in the smoking-room at Cranley, or in the precincts of any Club in London. I'm not going to quarrel, but what can you know in reality of the world? Some knowledge of slang is and always was part of a gentleman's education. Why, when the late Lord Lytton wrote 'Pelham' it was brought against him that 'his knowledge of flash was evidently purely superficial.' Flash, my sister, is merely recondite slang or thieves' *argot*."

"I can only say," returned Ellen, by no means mollified at the sharpness with which her brother was asserting his position as head of the family, " there is a savour of the race-course about your conversation which I, at all events, am not accustomed to."

Gerald bit his lip as the blood rushed into his face, and for a moment meditated an angry retort, but his new profession had schooled him severely in the disadvantage there is in loss of temper. He had not battled with equine infirmity of that nature without discovering the virtues of patience and "a calm sough." After a little he replied quietly,

"Don't be unkind, Nell. I started, remember, smashed, broken stock, lock, and barrel, as a Rockingham; that may be slang, but you understand it. Good! I have struck out my own line, and made a reputation under another name; that the world have discovered Jim Forrest and Gerald Rockingham to be one is no fault of mine. If you and mother feel so ashamed of me I'll pursue my career under the name of my adoption, but don't suppose, under any circumstances, that I shall not marry Dollie Greyson; because I shall, hap what may."

Miss Rockingham was not a little staggered at her brother's firmness. She had recognised for some time the change that had come over him, but she had thought the united entreaties of his mother and herself would have at least made him waver in his determination to marry Dollie Greyson. But it was evident he was shaken not one iota on this point. They had no choice between whether they would abandon Gerald or receive his wife, and as head of the family he had surely some right to dictate. Ellen was a little puzzled how to reply; her pride forbade her to give in to this brother younger than herself, while her common sense told her he had the right to select the woman he would marry, and meant to exercise it.

"I had thought you would have paid some attention to my wishes in such respect, Gerald," said Mrs. Rockingham, feebly.

"My dearest mother, I hope I shall always listen to your wishes about anything, but this is a thing a man must decide for himself."

Despite this being a question of serious disquiet to them, the two ladies could not refrain from exchanging a slight smile at hearing this dark-faced stripling, who had so suddenly arrogated to himself man's estate, pronounce his opinion in so decided a fashion.

"As I said before," continued Gerald, "not only do I love her very dearly, but I owe my present position entirely to her clear practical common sense. You may think that it is very easy for a Rockingham to get his living in this world, I can only say that, when it became necessary I should do it, I found Rockinghams considerably at a discount, and that except in my present profession I should be much puzzled how to earn thirty shillings a week."

"That is not exactly the question, Gerald. You have adopted this profession, and everybody knows it. It is much too late to say anything more about that, but we do urge you to pause before you take such an irrevocable step as getting married. Bemember, you can abandon a profession, but not a wife."

"I am not likely to change my determination," replied Gerald, quietly; "such training as I have gone through lately has strengthened my will as well as my muscles. An irresolute jockey would soon lose his riding. But if it will be any satisfaction to you to know that I don't mean marrying immediately you may have it. We can both afford to wait, and for the present I am bound to work hard at my profession; as I told you at my age it's impossible to say how long I may be able to continue it. The probability is I shall get too heavy in a few years. Mother, when may I bring my *fiancée* to see you?"

But, ere Mrs. Rockingham could answer, the door opened, and the servant announced "Mr. Thorndyke."

It was true that Ellen, after what had passed between them, had no cause to think that Mr. Thorndyke was in the least likely to intrude his advice upon Gerald; but she was decidedly non-plussed at the line John Thorndyke took up when, the first greetings over, she introduced him to her brother.

"How do you do, Mr. Rockingham?" said the genial rector. "I am delighted to make your acquaintance. We are all proud of you in Yorkshire, and so are your class all through England. It always does one good to see the gentleman hold his own with the professional. It shows there's grit left in us still."

"Thank you very much for your good opinion," replied Gerald, laughing; "but remember, I don't claim to be 'a gentleman,' I ride purely as a professional."

"I know," replied Thorndyke; "but a gentleman you are, and I feel quite sure will never forfeit that position. You are paid, and so indirectly are most gentlemen riders. The one difference is, *they* all take seven pounds' allowance as such, while you don't."

Gerald cast a triumphant look across at his sister; the name of John Thorndyke had cropped up not a little in that young lady's letters of late. Judging from past experience, Gerald had no doubt that what he had begun irreverently to term "Ellen's new pet parson" was of that extreme type that are merciless in their denunciations of the turf and all connected with it. Mr. Thorndyke's speech was a pleasant surprise to him. As he rose to go, he said simply :—

"I'm glad to have met you, Mr. Thorndyke, and I hope to see you again before long. You must excuse my running away now; I have lots to do, and very little time to do it in. Good-bye, Ellen; good-bye, mother dearest;" and, as he kissed her, Gerald whispered into her ear, "I shall bring Dollie to see you to-morrow morning."

CHAPTER VI.

"WILL YOU BE MY WIFE?"

"I CONGRATULATE you on your son, Mrs. Rockingham," said Mr. Thorndyke, as the door closed upon Gerald. "A fine, manly young fellow; and he has caught no taint of the profession he has embraced."

"I beg your pardon," interposed Ellen, a wee bit sharply. "His conversation was tolerably interlarded with horsey expressions before you came in. You only saw him for a minute or two, remember."

"What does that matter," rejoined the Rector. "A large proportion of the young gentlemen of the present day talk horse, and usually in exact inversion to their knowledge of the subject. He would probably have done that had he remained at Cambridge."

It was too provoking. John Thorndyke seemed to be holding a brief for Gerald; but, ere Ellen could reply, Mrs. Rockingham cut into the conversation.

"Ah! you do not know the worst," she said; "he contemplates marrying amongst these people."

"He is too young to think of that; not but what if he marries the right woman it very often steadies a young fellow, and is the making of him; but, when there is such difference of class, it's a doubtful experiment. A half-educated woman is apt to jar upon a refined man after the first. She is perpetually offending him unwittingly."

"I knew, Mr. Thorndyke, you would never approve of such a *mésalliance*," exclaimed Ellen, triumphantly.

"Forgive me; I don't altogether say that. I only say it's a dangerous experiment. It depends so much upon what the girl is like."

The two ladies exchanged glances, which said, "Shall we tell him?" and then Mrs. Rockingham rose, and, saying to her daughter, "You had better tell Mr. Thorndyke, and then perhaps he wouldn't mind saying to Gerald what he has just said to us. You will excuse me, as I have one or two little things to attend to."

"Let us hope it is not so bad as you think it, Mrs. Rockingham," said the Rector, as he opened the door for her. "Many girls in these days are educated what would have been thought far above their position forty years ago."

"You can't make a lady out of a trainer's daughter," retorted Mrs. Rockingham with no little asperity, as she swept from the apartment.

John Thorndyke bowed silently, and

then, taking a chair, waited until it should please Ellen to be communicative.

" This is very sad, very distressing for us, is it not ? " she said at length.

" Your brother is young, and as long as he is not actually married there is always considerable likelihood that he will change his mind," replied the rector, vaguely.

" I am afraid not. You don't know my brother—he is very obstinate when he has taken a thing into his head."

" Very resolute in purpose is, I fancy, more the term. Weak characters are obstinate. Your brother's career so far shows anything but weakness of character."

" Call it what you will," exclaimed Ellen, impatiently, " he is very fixed in his determination to marry this Dollie Greyson."

John Thorndyke was almost betrayed into a long whistle. " How very dull of me," he thought, "not to have guessed the riddle at once."

"Ah," he said dreamily at last, "if he is honestly in love with Miss Greyson I think the probability is he will be—well, we'll say obstinate."

"Why, what do you know about her?" exclaimed Ellen in amazement.

"Very little. I have only seen her two or three times in her uncle's shop, and she was such a pretty, graceful little girl that she attracted my attention, and I inquired who she was. Upon one occasion she served me with gloves or something, and in the few words that passed between us I recollect being much struck with her ladylike manner, so very superior to what one would have expected."

Really, Mr. Thorndyke was too bad. He had been looked to to, play in modified manner the part of Balaam, and, far from rebukes, he was dealing out nothing but approbation.

"Pray, have you ever seen the girl, Miss Rockingham?" inquired the rector, after a short pause.

"Yes," replied Ellen; "and I am bound to confess she is a pretty little thing; but," she added, with a shrug of her shoulders, "she is the daughter of William Greyson, the trainer, at one time my father's servant."

"It is awkward; but you know I don't attach quite so much importance to these things as you do. I have lived a good bit in the world, for when I had charge of a large parish in London I had most excellent introductions, and saw a good deal of society. The hardest workers find the most time for play. It's all method and arrangement. Well, Miss Rockingham, the prosperous butter-merchant's son of to-day goes to college, and let him only turn out a good fellow and his father die rich enough, mixes and marries in society."

"You don't mean to say," cried Ellen, "that you are advocating Gerald's marriage with this Miss Greyson?"

"No; certainly not. As I have said already, he is too young for one thing, nor do I know enough of the lady to be able to form an opinion. I only mean that from the little I have seen of her it is not nearly so bad as it sounds. You have not yet mastered the fusion of classes, which is one of the characteristics of the age."

"No; and I trust I never shall. I can't and won't believe it!" cried Ellen, passionately.

"Ah, well," said the rector, "you know the old proverb; 'None so blind,' &c. The representatives of the people might teach you that. Look at the present House of Commons, what an incongruous assembly it is! Men of birth, talent, and education sitting side by side with shopkeepers, &c., and the result is that one man of transcendent genius rules it with a rod of iron, makes it, when he chooses to take up that rod, cower like naughty children, and yield to his whims and caprices whatever they may be. Democracy is always dangerously near autocracy, and no man since the days of the Tudors was ever so absolutely ruler of England."

Ellen, however she disagreed with him, was always deeply interested when John Thorndyke talked in this way, and of late the girl had lost her self-reliance, and caught herself wondering whether it was not more likely that John Thorndyke, with all his knowledge of life, learning, and common sense, should be a better judge of these things than herself. Canon Durnford, too, although he laughingly repudiated sharing the Rector of St. Margaret's extreme views, indirectly confirmed them to a certain extent.

Still, listening with interest to Mr.

Thorndyke's Radical theories was a very different thing from welcoming Dollie Greyson as a sister.

But the rector had stopped talking, and after a slight pause broke into a low laugh, as he said:

"Ten thousand pardons, Miss Rockingham. I had no business to hold forth in that fashion, but once give a man a chance to ride his hobby, and it's sure to get away with him. Forgive me. Upon my word," he continued, breaking into a peal of laughter, "I really thought I was on 'the stump.'"

"No, Mr. Thorndyke, I like to hear you talk, little as I agree with you, but we women, as a rule, are all Conservatives to the backbone. We dread our advanced sisters, and want neither votes nor seats in Parliament. I for one think the 'Mrs. Jellabys' of the world do no good in their generation, and may well leave such work to their male belongings."

"Perhaps you are right. At all events, Radical as I am, that is my opinion also. But do you want my advice about your brother's engagement?"

"Ah, Mr. Thorndyke, you will speak to him and point out to him the mistake he is making, won't you?" cried Ellen.

"No, not at all. I wash my hands of it. I simply recommend you to make no further objection. Your brother, from what I see of him, is little likely to be swayed by any one in this matter. To oppose him means to quarrel with him, and, if anything, hurry his marriage. Rest contented then. The girl is pretty and ladylike. It is quite possible, when I know her, I shall congratulate you most heartily on your sister-in-law."

A sudden thought flashed through Ellen's mind. Could Mr. Thorndyke contemplate some such marriage as Gerald. Was he advocating his own cause while pretending that he could not see anything much to be distressed about in her brother's engagement. A strange feeling of weariness, for which she herself could hardly account, came across her at this idea. She had never heard of Mr. Thorndyke being particular in his attentions to any lady in York, but he was just the man to be struck with any case of devotion and self-sacrifice amongst the poorer of his parishioners, and, if the maiden were comely, quite capable of asking her to share his home, with very little heed as to what the world would say of it.

"Would you make such a marriage yourself?" she asked, a little shyly, after a long pause.

"No," replied the Rector, bluntly.

"Then, Mr. Thorndyke," exclaimed Ellen, "how can you support my brother in his preposterous folly?"

"I would not myself make such a marriage, because I hope to marry a woman of a very different station," and the quiet, resolute tones in which the answer was given, and the straight glance of John Thorndyke's blue eyes into her own, told the girl at once who that woman was.

Ellen's heart gave a great jump; she recognised now why she had felt uneasy at the idea of John Thorndyke marrying, but, though she had conceived a great, liking and respect for the rector, she honestly had never yet thought of him in the light of a possible lover. But she recovered her presence of mind in a few seconds, and replied,

"That sounds to me an additional reason why you should expostulate with my brother."

"Never mind your brother just now. I've a question to ask you on my own account. You've known me now over a twelvemonth, Miss Rockingham, and I have learnt in that time to love you very dearly. Will you be my wife? Stop!" he continued, seeing that she was about to interrupt him, "don't think that we differ very much in our views of life or religion. We both wish to do such good as may lie within our power, and tolerance should be a cardinal point in all creeds. If you love me there will speedily be little difference of opinion between us."

Suddenly Ellen rose to her feet. "Mr. Thorndyke," she said, "you have paid me the greatest compliment a man can pay a woman, and for that I thank you; but I have too great a regard and esteem for you to answer your question without some little consideration. You have taken me by surprise. I must have time to think whether I could be the wife I wish to be to you."

"I am quite satisfied on that point," rejoined Thorndyke, smiling, "only say you will be my wife and I am quite willing to chance your being a good one."

"Please let me go now, I want to be alone and think," exclaimed Ellen, resisting her lover's attempt to detain her hand.

"It shall be as you will," he replied, releasing her, "although I had hoped to have won a consent from your lips this morning, but, Ellen, you won't keep me long in suspense?"

"No, you shall hear from me to-morrow morning without fail. For the present, good-bye," and the rector felt that he was dismissed.

John Thorndyke did not feel much disturbed that he had failed to obtain a final answer that morning. He understood Miss Rockingham's character too well. She would have been prompt enough if she had meant to say no. Most women when they debate about accepting a man rarely come to that conclusion. The girl with her somewhat rigid principles had unconsciously made it very difficult for herself to give Thorndyke a negative answer. She had great contempt for the littleness of coquetry, and there would have been a spice of that in keeping a straight-forward, honest gentleman in suspense, if she had much doubt about what her decision would be. The rector felt well satisfied with his morning's work as he strolled homewards, and his thoughts now drifted into some mundane reflections about his professional prospects. The first five years of his ministry had been passed in the quiet country rectory in which he had succeeded his father; but when the almost simultaneous death of his mother and sister released him from keeping the home to which they were so wedded over their heads, he at once applied for metropolitan preferment, and was quickly installed in one of those large East-end parishes that often prove the stepping-stone to promotion. From thence he had been transferred to York at his own request, finding the sickly London atmosphere, after three years, began telling on a man so used to the fresh pure country air and a healthy country life as he had been.

John Thorndyke knew that he stood well with the chiefs of the Church, despite his somewhat peculiar views, and that he might count upon promotion in some shape before long, and he thought now would be a fitting time to jog their memories.

CHAPTER VII.

POOR OLD DANCER.

The two ladies in St. Leonard's Place were a little at cross purposes that night. Mrs. Rockingham was absorbed in the idea of receiving the bride of her son's election to-morrow morning, while Ellen, it need scarcely be said, with a lover of her own to say yea or nay to, could hardly be expected to keep a proposed sister-in-law in mind.

"It will be a terrible thing if we don't like her," murmured Mrs. Rockingham at length.

"I wonder what Gerald will say to it," responded Ellen, who had just awoke to the fact that her brother was head of the family, and that it behoved her to acquaint him at once with her engagement.

"Yes, it will be very awkward," rejoined Mrs. Rockingham. "He is so masterful and hot-tempered, and yet if we don't like her it's absurd to pretend we do."

The termination of this last remark recalled Ellen from her dreamland just as she was about indignantly to protest against Mr. Thorndyke being called hot-tempered.

"Don't worry yourself about it beforehand, mamma. We are bound to accept this girl for Gerald's sake if he insists on marrying her. In the meantime, remember, I have seen Miss Greyson, and can assure you she is quite presentable, and rather pretty. Some people, I dare say, would admire her a good deal."

John Thorndyke was right: if Ellen loved him there was likely to be very little differing between them: the suddenness with which she had changed sides, and adopted his view with regard to Gerald's marriage, promised well for the answer she should give him to-morrow.

Mrs. Rockingham was a woman who had all her life been accustomed to lean upon some one. During her married life she had depended entirely upon her husband. At his death Gerald, while he stayed with them, had assumed the reins of government, no little to the astonishment of his self-reliant sister, but when he disappeared Ellen had, of course, stepped into his place. If Mrs. Rockingham was much astonished at Ellen's change of front, she nevertheless, after a long palaver, in which the opinion of John Thorndyke was freely quoted, perfectly acquiesced in it, and it was decided that Dollie should be welcomed as Gerald's chosen bride when she called. Further, Ellen confided to her mother that John

Thorndyke had asked her to marry him, and that before she went to bed she meant to write and tell him she was his when it pleased him to take her; all which ended, as may be supposed, in a comfortable cry, and then the two ladies retired to rest thoroughly happy.

Mrs. and Miss Rockingham were not women to do things by halves, and, when Gerald and his *fiancée* arrived the next morning in St. Leonard's Place, they welcomed the latter with great cordiality. Dollie had come prepared, if she could, to make friends with Mrs. Rockingham, and to maintain a polite neutrality with Ellen, but the latter had completely disarmed her by the warmth of her greeting. She seized the earliest opportunity of drawing Dollie a little apart, and then said :

"I want you to let bygones be bygones. You must forgive me if, in the first instance, I did not like the idea of having you for a sister-in-law. You must make allowances for the bitterness of having lost our old home, the home of our race for the last two hundred years and more. You must remember that the Rockinghams of Cranley were wont in their pride to think themselves mates for any in the land, and that a woman's first idea would be that Gerald should restore the fortunes of his house by marriage; and lastly, bear in mind, no sister ever thought any one good enough for an only brother."

All this said in Ellen's most winning tones was quite enough to break down the reserve in which Dollie had entrenched herself.

"Of course you didn't like it," she replied, shyly. "I always told him you wouldn't; but then, you see, I love him."

"Yes, and you must recollect, Dollie—I may call you so, may I not?—that I did not know in those days all you had done for him. It was you put him in the way of earning his own living—not quite the one we should have chosen, perhaps; but he is such a success, no Yorkshire girl, who belonged to him, could help being proud of him."

"Yes, Miss Rockingham," cried the girl, as her eyes sparkled and her cheeks flushed with triumph, "he won the Two Thousand on the wickedest colt we ever had at Riddleton."

"He always could ride," replied Ellen, "and I am told that you are as good as he in the hunting-field?"

"I don't mind where I follow Gerald," observed the girl, naïvely.

Miss Rockingham had some little difficulty in suppressing a smile as the thought flashed across her that Dollie had followed her brother to some purpose, but she wanted to become friends with her, and knew that was not a subject to jest upon at present.

"You pass a good deal of your time in York, do you not?" inquired Ellen.

"I have done so. You see I am passionately fond of music, and I also wanted to learn a good many things that girls of my station don't usually aspire to. I have been at York chiefly for masters. At Riddleton," she continued, laughing merrily, "we only teach riding and the management of the dairy."

Neither Gerald nor Miss Greyson made the slightest allusion to his novitiate. It was not that he cared much about its being known. It was all past and gone now, but he thought it would pain his mother and sister to learn that he had passed some little time as a stable-boy. At present they never questioned but what he had been requested as a particular favour to ride in the Two Thousand Guineas in consequence of his prowess with the York and Ainsty, and then, at Dollie's suggestion, had adopted it as a profession. After a short talk with Gerald, Mrs. Rockingham, who has been agreeably surprised at the appearance of her future daughter-in-law, comes across to improve her acquaintance with Dollie, and thereby occasions a change of partners.

"Well, Nell," said Gerald, as his sister took a chair beside him, "I hope you will get on with my wife."

"I think so," replied Ellen, "at all events we have one point in common, to wit, our love for your precious self. But, Gerald, how long are you going to stay with us?"

"I must leave this afternoon. I have some business at Riddleton I want to see old Greyson about, and then I must hurry back to Newmarket. I had great trouble to snatch these two days as it was. I should soon lose my business if I didn't attend to it, and you know it is the height of the racing season."

"I have something to tell you before you go," said Miss Rockingham, speaking slowly. "Yesterday, after you left, Mr.

Thorndyke asked me to marry him. I asked for a few hours to think over my answer, and this morning I wrote to say I would."

"And now you come to me as head of the family, Nell, to ask my consent," exclaimed Gerald, laughing. "My dear sister, you have my heartiest congratulations. Thorndyke seems, from the little I have seen of him, a right good sort, and, at all events, he won't be ashamed of his brother-in-law Jim Forrest."

"Ah, Gerald," replied Ellen, as she yielded both her hands to his brotherly clasp, "you must make allowances for my oldfashioned prejudices. If I have overcome in some measure the creed in which I was brought up, it is due to Mr. Thorndyke's teaching."

"Ah! you've learnt at last that the world can get on without Rockinghams. Yes; it's a sad thing to say in these days of high education, but I owe my present comfortable position and income not to Harrow and Cambridge, but to the accident of being of small stature, and to the teaching of old Western, the studgroom at Cranley. By the way, I suppose you know the old place is to be sold in September?"

"No; of course I knew it must be, but had not heard when it was to take place. It really makes no difference, and yet somehow, Gerald, it will seem a wrench. You have no idea, I suppose, who will buy it?"

"No; we have failed to find a purchaser for it. To be disposed of by public auction is its fate now."

"You will be up here for the races this time, I suppose?" said Ellen, inquiringly.

"Yes. I made the mistake last year of being ashamed of my trade. I shall not fall into it again. As luck would have it, no harm was done; but it is much too risky an experiment to repeat. Besides, my *incognito* is at an end."

"Yes. And Gerald, dear, I'll own to very mixed feelings about it. I am half-proud, half-ashamed, and mamma is much the same — proud of your skill in the saddle, but a little sore that a Rockingham should be riding for hire."

"Nonsense, Nell; one might as well be a jockey as a cab proprietor, and two or three of the nobility are in that line. But it's time I was going. Good-bye; good-bye mother. You'll come to the station and see me off, Dollie?"

"It's nothing near as bad as I feared," said Mrs. Rockingham, as the door closed behind her son and his intended. "The girl is well enough, and would pass muster anywhere, but the connection is awkward."

"I don't suppose we shall be expected to see anything of Mr. William Greyson," replied Ellen, rather loftily. "We accept

Gerald's wife, but we are not called upon to swallow her family. I told Gerald I was going to be married, mamma."

"And he?"

"Congratulated me as heartily as a man immersed in his own love affairs can be expected to do," replied Ellen.

Gerald was rather silent on his way to the station. He was turning over in his mind two rather important suggestions that had been made to him during his present flying visit to York. One was that of Mr. Writson, namely, that he should endeavour to get Lord Whitby to exercise some pressure on Cuthbert Ellison with regard to those promissory notes. That the concensus of public opinion was more likely to bring a man situated like Elliston to terms than legal measures the old lawyer knew well, to say nothing of there being no legal measures possible in this case. Gerald knew he could depend upon Writson's opinion, and, though his distaste for invoking foreign aid in his family affairs was such that had it only concerned himself he would have undoubtedly let the whole matter go, still he recognised that it behoved him to recover as much of the money as he could for his mother and sister. Secondly, there was Dollie's idea that a big race might be got out of "the Dancer," and it was to sound Bill Greyson on that point that he was now going to Riddleton.

"Good-bye, dearest," he said, as the train glided into the station. "You will see me again in a few weeks, for I mean to gratify your curiosity and ride at York this time."

"Mind you do, and win," replied Dollie, with a bright little nod of adieu. "Give father and mother my love, and don't forget to write."

As he sped on his way to Riddleton Gerald's mind was busy revolving what *coup* on earth it was possible to pull off with the Dancing Master. He believed implicitly that when the brute chose to try he was a very great horse, that he not only had a tremendous turn of speed, but, what rarely goes with it, great lasting capabilities. Gerald was bent upon playing for a big stake, and it grew upon him more and more as he travelled on that this queer-tempered iron-grey four-year-old was the instrument for his purpose. It was quite true that no more dangerous horse to place your money on could be found, as Sir Marmaduke had discovered to his cost in the Hunt Cup at Ascot, and Gerald was quite aware of what the Dancing Master had once or twice done with Pibroch and Bushranger on the training-ground to justify that plunging on the baronet's part. Had the horse in the race run within 7lb. of his home performance he would have won easily, but then, again, that little infirmity that wrecks both men and horses intervened, and his " beastly temper" led to his discomfiture. Still, this was just the animal to " go for the gloves" on. What may be termed his criminal record was so bad that he was sure to be allotted a very light weight in any handicap he might be now entered for, and the Ring would be bound to field strongly against a horse whose irritable temperament was so well known, and who had had already on more than one occasion proved so staunch a friend to them. The immediate question naturally was, What did Bill Greyson mean to do with the Dancing Master, now, according to Dollie, returned to him to do with as he willed? It was not likely the trainer would give up all hope concerning him as yet, more especially when it was borne in mind that he had been an amazingly profitable horse to Mr. Bill Greyson, and might yet, with luck and judicious handling, be sold to considerable advantage.

Gerald was a little non-plussed on arriving at the Moor Farm with his reception. The trainer seemed very pleased to see him, but welcomed him hat in hand, and as " Mr. Rockingham."

" Very glad, indeed, to see you, sir. The late squire was a liberal master to me at one time, and it was not altogether my fault that he took his horses away from Riddleton. But what will you do Mr. Rockingham? Will you walk through the stables first, and then have some lunch, or will you have something to eat at once ? "

" Thanks, Greyson. I am very much pressed for time, so, if you will let me, I'll have something to eat first, and I can talk to you at the same time. Dollie tells me you have got the Dancer back upon your hands."

"Yes; Sir Marmaduke got such a sickener over the Hunt Cup that he sent the horse back the following week," replied the trainer, sententiously. "It was enough to make him; but you rode in the race, sir, and know all about it."

"Yes, and I did think it was going to be his day. I thought Blackton had us all safe, when the Dancer suddenly shut up, without rhyme or reason."

"Yes; he'll never get a better chance, and it's hopeless to train him. He's been a good horse to me, but I don't think any one else will ever get a turn out of him."

"What do you mean to do with him?" inquired Gerald.

"Sell him the very first opportunity, and with a view to that I shall enter him for the two big back-end handicaps. After his exhibition at Ascot he is safe to be thrown in, and he may catch somebody's fancy who wants to go for a big stake without very much risk. As I said before, he's been a good horse to me, but *I* don't trust him again."

Curious — "a big stake without very much risk!" Was not this the very chance Gerald was seeking, and two very good judges had foreseen that the Dancing Master was a possible medium through which that desirable consummation might be achieved. Sir Marmaduke, in the first instance, had hit off what Gerald began to believe was the necessary combination when he had leased the horse with a view to winning the Leger; to wit, that the Dancing Master would run honest in his (Gerald's) hands, and no one else's. Now Greyson saw a great opportunity in either the Cesarewitch or Cambridgeshire, but, strange to say, that it was essential Gerald should ride did not seem to have occurred to the astute trainer. But the idea was rapidly spreading through Gerald's mind that this might really be so, and that in his hands the horse might once more do his best, and carry off another big race.

"There are worse speculations about than that," he said, at length, "and it won't signify however light the weight they put upon him. He has got such a name as a bad-tempered coward, that nothing but an enormous outlay of money will ever make him a strong favourite. The public have lost faith in him."

"And so has the owner and trainer," said Greyson, laughing. "Would you like to see him, sir?"

"Yes, by all means. I wonder whether he'll remember me?"

"I'll pound it he will. They've wonderful memories, have horses, and strongish likes and dislikes. I'd a line from Pipes," continued the trainer, as he led the way towards the stables to the left of the house, "when he sent the Dancer back, 'Put up who you like on him,' he wrote, 'but never Blackton; the horse can't bear him, and has tried to savage him more than once. If Sir Marmaduke would give him another chance I should advise another jockey.'"

As Greyson opened the door of his box the Dancing Master turned his head, cast a sinister glance at the new comers as though recommending them to keep themselves to themselves as far as he was concerned, and then resumed some apparently elaborate researches in his manger. The horse certainly took no notice of Gerald, but no sooner did it hear his whisper of "Poor old Dancer," than it turned its head sharply with a short grunt of satisfaction, and unmistakably gazed wistfully towards the corner from which the voice had come.

"Go up to him, sir; only be careful," said the trainer.

Gerald walked boldly up to the horse's head, once more whispering "Poor old Dancer!" as he did so. The grey laid back his ears viciously as he approached, but upon hearing his voice the second time apparently changed his mind, and rubbed his black muzzle against his visitor's waistcoat when he reached his shoulder.

"Well, sir," said the trainer, no little astonished; "I never saw him do that before to any one. Did he ever to you when you looked after him?"

"Yes, but only now and then. Still, he always seemed to take notice when I talked to him; though," added Gerald, laughing, "he didn't take much heed of what I said. He looks well."

"He's always well," returned Greyson; "never been sick nor sorry yet. I wish some of the others had his constitution. Now, here's Caterham," he exclaimed, as he threw open the door of an adjoining box, "a clipper, but as delicate a horse as ever I trained. We couldn't make anything of him last antumn; but he's wonderfully well now, and should do your cousin, Mr. Elliston, a rare turn whenever his time comes."

"Which will be about October, I suppose," said Gerald.

"I can't say, sir. Mr. Elliston is not communicative, nor are his orders open secrets even when I get them."

Gerald took the hint, and asked no further questions. He strolled carelessly through the stables, and honestly complimented the trainer upon the blooming condition of more than one of his charges. As they walked back to the house he said carelessly, "I suppose you'll keep the Dancer in strong work?"

"I shall train him so that he can easily be wound up for either Cesarewitch or Cambridgeshire, if any one wants to buy him with a view to those handicaps; but as my horse he'll start for neither."

"Well, Greyson, thanks very much. The nags, take 'em all round, look wonderfully well; and now I must be off. I shall hardly catch the train as it is."

"Oh, yes, you will, sir. My trap's at the door, and you've a good five minutes in hand."

"Good-bye. Kind regards to Mrs. Greyson, and say how sorry I am to have missed her," said Gerald, as he leaped into the dog-cart.

CHAPTER VIII.

CRANLEY GOES TO THE HAMMER.

The weeks slipped by since Gerald's return to Newmarket, and as yet he had no opportunity of unburdening himself to Lord Whitby, and ascertaining whether the peer would exercise such social pressure as lay at his command to compel Cuthbert Elliston to restore some of the money which he had borrowed from Alister Rockingham. Lord Whitby, indeed, had only attended one race-meeting of late, and that was Goodwood, where Gerald had no opportunity of speaking to him in private. York Races had come round again, and Lord Whitby had announced his intention of being there to see his horses run, and then perhaps Gerald might find the desired opportunity. The peer was in rare good humour; the year had been a procession of triumphs so far. The Great Yorkshire Stakes and sundry other valuable prizes at Doncaster and Newmarket were apparently at his mercy, and he bid fair to be returned at the head of the poll when the return of the principal winners of the season should be issued. York race-week, too, was to see the irrevocable sale of Cranley, and Gerald reflected ruefully that, though he had thought his *coup* out, and was quite determined to play for it, yet, if it came off, it would be too late to save " The Chase." He had resolved, if he could, to try and win the Cambridgeshire with the Dancing Master, arguing that no weight there was any probability of his being allotted could prevent him if only the horse chose to do his best. Still, this experiment could not be tried till the end of October, and the lands of the Rockinghams were to come to the hammer in August. Gerald could see no possibility of saving the home of his ancestors. Men to advance money on the possibility of a big race coming off in one's favour are not to be met with; and that was about the sum total of security that Gerald could proffer for such a sum as would enable him to redeem Cranley Chase.

What Greyson might want for the Dancing Master was a thing that Gerald had never troubled himself to consider. It was no part of his scheme to buy the horse; he considered that such money as he could spare he should want for betting purposes, and that he would be able to induce the trainer to run him in consideration of being put on to win a comfortable stake. Gerald's idea was to back the horse very quietly and gradually as soon as betting began about the Cambridgeshire, but not to disclose his plan to Greyson until he had got the best part of the sum he meant to speculate with duly invested. The one flaw in his scheme was this: there was always the possibility of some one buying the Dancing Master on the same speculation, and not caring particularly about "Jim Forrest's" riding for him, and it was quite part of Gerald's belief that nobody but himself could induce the horse to do his best. He was young, and who shall blame him if his head was just a little turned with success? Besides, had not his late employer, Sir Marmaduke, taken the same view of the case, and was not Sir Marmaduke accounted exceedingly wise among the younger generation of turfites?

Gerald went up to York, as in duty bound, with slightly mingled feelings. He had schooled himself to drop all false pride about his profession by this, but he did feel seriously anxious to acquit himself with distinction on what might be termed his own dunghill. Half the people on the Knavesmire, he was aware, would know that "Jim Forrest" was young Rockingham. Besides, would not the lady of his love be there to see, and it would never do to go down in the lists before all this goodly company. He was to ride, moreover, a red-hot favourite for the Yorkshire Stakes belonging to Lord Whitby, which the prophets declared to a man could not lose, and of the mendacious utterances of racing seers Gerald by this had seen something. When the prophets are in unison there is more often trouble in store for the favourite than not. Then again, the sale of the Cranley estates was to take place that week, which would call additional attention to the last scion of the Rockinghams. He had, of course, quite made up his mind to all this, but it was nevertheless a little trying up in his "ain countree." However, he consoled himself with the reflection that everybody knew his story now, and, as for nerve, well, it had never failed him on a race-course yet.

But Gerald was destined to hear a bit of news on his arrival at York that roused his ire not a little, and determined him to lose no time in bringing any pressure he could command to bear upon Cuthbert Elliston. He was having his dinner quietly in the coffee-room of Harker's Hotel when his attention was attracted by hearing his own name mentioned by one of two individuals who were dining in the adjoining box.

"Yes," continued the speaker, "he was a rare sportsman was poor Squire Rockingham, and carried on the game merrily. He was a bold better, too, terrible bold, but the Ring outstayed him, as they always do when men dash it down as he did."

"Ah, all Cranley's to come to the hammer; there's a nice bit of grazing land. I mean to have it if it goes reasonable. Lot 34; here you are," and the speaker evidently referred to a sale catalogue.

"I wonder who'll buy the Chase itself," said the first speaker.

"Well, it's a bit of a secret, so you must not go gabbling it all about the city; but Lawyer Pearson always manages what law business I have. I consulted him about this bit of land I want to buy on Friday. Now, I chance to have a nephew in the office, and I often have a chat with him, and we got talking over the big Cranley sale. He told me they had three or four commissions to buy at a price, and one, he said, from the family."

"Ah, that'd be for the Chase. I'll be main glad if the Rockinghams can contrive to keep the Chase, and so'll many another."

"Oh, but this chap isn't a Rockingham

exactly. He's one of the family, no doubt, but one the country side don't care much about. Yorkshire was no better for Cuthbert Elliston's winning the Leger, nor the poor squire either that ever I heard."

"No; I don't think folk will be much pleased at Mr. Elliston taking Alister Rockingham's place."

"No; he's a cross-bred 'un, that Elliston. In the days the poor Squire had winners, half Yorkshire was in the swim, but Mr. Elliston and Pearson always eat their own cake, and don't want any one to help them."

And then the speakers dismissed the Cranley sale from their conversation, and became immersed in elaborate calculations about weights and previous performances, all bearing more or less on the forthcoming week's racing.

Gerald drew his breath hard as he listened to the above. What! Cuthbert

Elliston, his detested cousin, master of the Chase! Could Heaven look calmly down upon such iniquity? The man who had robbed his father sitting down in that much-loved home upon the proceeds of his frauds seemed to Gerald too monstrous. It mattered little who had the Chase, but any one rather than Cuthbert Elliston. Nothing would grate upon the feelings of him and his more than the idea of his cousin installed at the Chase. If he could prevent that, he would at any cost, but the question was, could he? He was in no position to bid against Cuthbert for its possession, and, if his cousin could afford to buy it, who was to prevent him? He must see Writson to-morrow before the racing began, and even as the idea passed through his mind it was almost effaced by the rapid afterthought, what was the good of seeing Writson? Then he resolved to go to bed betimes, and see Lord Whitby the first thing next morning. If that nobleman chose to help him, he might at all events prevent Elliston buying the Chase.

True to his resolution Gerald presented himself at the Black Swan the next morning, and sent up his name to Lord Whitby, with a request that he would see him for a few minutes. It rather annoyed Gerald to find that he attracted not a little attention among the servants and loungers, but he had made up his mind that must be. His story was, of course, public property now, and there were plenty of people in York who knew young Rockingham by sight, as well as many more who as racegoers were familiar with the features of Jim Forrest the jockey. However, a few minutes, and a waiter requests him to step upstairs, and ushers him into a sitting-room, where he finds Lord Whitby lounging over the *débris* of his breakfast.

" Sit down, Mr. Rockingham," said that

nobleman, greeting him with that rather studied politeness, which was one of his most marked attributes, until such time as circumstances stirred the tempest of his wrath, when his language was apt to be more forcible than polished. "I am afraid this sale must grate upon your feelings rather, but you have no doubt made up your mind to it as inevitable."

"Yes, my lord," replied Gerald, who never permitted himself to forget that he was speaking to his employer; "but I have heard a bit of news about it that has annoyed me much since I have been in York, and that is that my cousin, Cuthbert Elliston, contemplates buying my old home "

"I don't think the neighbourhood will welcome him very cordially as the successor of Alister Rockingham," replied Lord Whitby, contemptuously. "Your cousin is neither popular nor in very good odour amongst the *gentlemen* on the turf.

I don't think much of Mr. Elliston; in fact, sir, I consider him a d——d scoundrel," concluded the peer, who detested the man, and had been rather outspoken concerning some of his more questionable practices.

"You can't think worse of him, my lord, than I do," replied Gerald. "He had a principal share in my father's ruin. Since I have been a jockey I have heard the story of Phaeton's Leger. I hold at the present moment a sheaf of his bills which my poor father had to meet representing several thousand pounds, and which he has the audacity to wish to compound for one, knowing how we have been left. I know, moreover, on more than one occasion that his manœuvring with the horses almost compromised my father's honour. Greyson told me the other day that it was not altogether his fault that my father left him. Not altogether, no! It was because he was weak enough to follow Cuthbert Elliston's orders."

"You're right, Rockingham, by heaven you are!" exclaimed the peer, passionately. "That's the whole story of your father's death and ruin, for it was the utter smash that broke his heart at last. No! Sooner than that d——d black-hearted thief should step into his shoes I'll buy the Chase myself. I don't want it, but," and here the speaker launched a mighty torrent of execrations which culminated in the peroration that "a white-livered skunk should never have it."

But at last the choleric nobleman calmed down, and made Gerald tell him all about the bills, and Cuthbert Elliston's conduct concerning them; even the bitter advice Elliston had tendered just after Alister Rockingham's funeral Lord Whitby managed to draw from the young fellow.

"Did he know who you were when you

rode his horse in the Two Thousand last year?"

"No; but of course he recognised me as soon as I had won, and immediately gave orders that I was to be sent away from Riddleton. That is the sole guerdon I received at his hands for my success."

"Ah, I fancy he didn't profit much by it, and that probably he would have been just as well pleased if you hadn't won."

"At all events he's repented once of his advice; when I beat him on Sir Marmaduke's horse for the Goodwood Stakes last year I know it was a costly race for him."

"Well, Rockingham, I'll do the best I can for you, but rest assured of one thing, Cuthbert Elliston shall never reign at Cranley. Just write me down your solicitor's address."

Gerald did so, and then thanked his lordship and departed gaily. It was the presage of a most successful week. He not only brought off the Great Yorkshire Stakes successfully for his employer, but never rode more brilliantly, and carried off some four or five minor stakes to boot. In one instance his triumph was notably due to his fine horsemanship.

But if it was a successful week for Gerald it was a most disastrous one for Elliston. Riddleton rather laid itself out for handicaps, and had certainly flattered itself that some two or three of these races lay at its mercy when it saw the weights allotted to its representatives. But the stable was dead out of luck, and failed upon each occasion to achieve the expected victory. Even the cautious Sam Pearson looked glum as he saw the accumulation of figures on the debit scale of his betting-book, while, as for Elliston, who had looked forward to his week's winnings to materially assist him towards the purchase of the Chase, he could not control his ill-humour, which a communication from Pearson did not tend to mitigate.

Whether under the circumstances Elliston would have persisted in his mad design is open to question, but a visit Mr. Writson paid Pearson on the Wednesday morning effectually settled Mr. Elliston's pretensions in the matter. Writson said he was instructed by Lord Whitby to let Mr. Elliston know, through his solicitor, that as an old friend of Alister Rockingham's he intended to exercise all the social pressure he could bring to bear to wring from Elliston the sum he was still in honour indebted to the Rockingham family. "Further," continued Pearson, "I was clearly given to understand that if you attempted to bid for the Chase the story would be widely spread through York that you were buying the house with the money the squire had lent you, and that, moreover, you would have to encounter a pretty stiff opposition to boot."

"That means that old Whitby will bid against me, I suppose," interrupted Elliston, roughly. "It's useless to measure purses with him, or else it's little I care for his threats in the other direction."

But Cuthbert Elliston knew that he lied when he said this, and so did his chum and partner, Pearson. Elliston's reputation was too shady to risk a row with such a relentless and powerful opponent as Lord Whitby, and so it came to pass that when the Chase was brought to the hammer it pleased that wealthy and eccentric nobleman, in high good humour with his York victories, to buy it, with no very clear idea of what he was going to do with it after he had got it.

CHAPTER IX.

DOLLIE TURNS SCHOOLMISTRESS.

York had made the confederates take counsel as to how its disasters were to be retrieved. Elliston in particular had been a very heavy loser, dropping, indeed, a considerable portion of the winnings of the year. He was always a rather dashing bettor when in funds, and in his impatience to increase his capital had conducted his speculations on a more extensive scale than usual. He was, moreover, by no means so impassive in the hour of defeat as his more cautious partner, who usually bore victory or reverses with stoical indifference. It may be that he was conscious of a second string to his bow, and felt that, when he had failed to get the better of the bookmakers, his clients, at all events, were not likely to escape with their quill-feathers.

Elliston was of that type of man unbearable in either fortune. Exultant, hectoring, and blustering when in luck; morose, cynical, and sarcastic when the capricious goddess abandoned him. He was further embittered by another message he received from Mr. Writson, that, though in consideration of his reverses at York social pressure would not be immediately brought to bear upon him, yet, unless he made arrangements to pay two thousand in liquidation of those bills, the story of the transaction would be made public, and a hint was thrown out that he was at all events the owner of some valuable horses, which might be realised.

"That old brute, Whitby, is pulling the strings, of course, Sam. He must do his worst. I've not the money to spare at present," snarled Elliston when Pearson delivered his message.

"Yes, and when you have got hold of a couple of thousand pounds I recommend you to come to terms. Whitby's a dangerous man for a turfite to quarrel with, and carries too many guns for you or me."

"Nonsense! Don't bother any more about the bills. You had far more of poor Alister's money, if the truth was told, than I had."

"That's got nothing to do with it. What I received was in the way of business. However, the bills are your affair, not mine, and you know best what the consequences will be to you if the story comes out. I should call it awkward if it threatened me, and should imagine it was worse for you," rejoined the attorney.

"At all events, it isn't pressing just now, and, if our present luck lasts, I bid fair to be tolerably indifferent to public opinion before the year's out," replied Elliston.

The scene of the above conversation was that very room at the Salutation at Doncaster in which it had been decided to win the Leger two years before with Phaeton if possible. Elliston had won and lost a good deal of money since then, but probably was at the present moment very little richer than before that great *coup*. Money made by gambling is ever-shifting as a quicksand, pouring from one pocket into another with feverish haste, as if bitten by the restlessness of those who win and lose it. After studying a sheet of paper intently for some minutes Elliston exclaimed petulantly:

"Except our confounded luck I can't see anything to beat Caterham in either handicap."

"No," returned Pearson, who was occupied in a similar study of the weights for the Cesarewitch and Cambridgeshire. "Seven stone twelve on a five-year-old that was good enough to win the Two Thousand at three can't be called excessive."

"No; and they've given him five pounds less in the long race, which shows that they think as we do that he's better at one mile than two. We must go over to Riddleton, and have a talk with Greyson; and, if we only find the horse going on as well as he was the last time I was there, we'll slip him for the Cambridgeshire."

"Yes," said Pearson, "he ought to have a great chance; but here's another Two Thousand winner at the same weight. Mr. Greyson's Dancing Master, four-year-old, seven twelve."

"Bah! a brute with a temper like that it don't much matter how little they put upon his back, besides, we can always give Greyson orders not to run him," rejoined Elliston. "Sir Marmaduke's done with him, you know."

"True! his temper's quite gone, I fancy. Still, he's always just the beggar to upset calculations. There ought to be a law prohibiting the running of such horses as him, for the protection of owners and backers. However, I don't suppose Greyson has any serious intention of starting him."

"No; however, I shall veto that if he has. We'll go over to Riddleton on Monday and have a confab with him about it, and then trust me to slowly work the commission. We ought to take thirty thousand out of the Ring easily over this."

"Providing it comes off; but remember we're not the only people who have laid themselves out for the same little game," rejoined cautious Sam Pearson. "There's a good many just as sanguine as ourselves, and with cards up their sleeve that we know nothing about."

Still, the more the confederates talked over the thing the firmer they became in their conviction that they had a very big chance of winning the Cambridgeshire, and before their conference broke up it had been decided between them that, unless Greyson showed good cause why they should not run Caterham for that race, run they would, and give the Ring reason to remember it if it came off.

But, as Pearson had suggested, there were many inquisitive eyes scanning that mystical problem, the weights for the Autumn Handicaps, and it was with a grin of intense satisfaction that Elliston noted, ere the Doncaster Meeting terminated, a strong disposition on the part of the public to back Caterham for the Cesarewitch.

"We'll let 'em burn their fingers pretty badly over that, Sam," said that astute and unscrupulous tactician, "and then they'll leave chestnuts of ours alone for the future, and let us take 'em out of the fire for ourselves."

Betting, in the days of our story, commenced on the two great Autumn Handicaps at Newmarket considerably earlier than it does at present, and two people noted with no little interest that the Dancing Master was ever and again backed at long shots for the Cambridgeshire. Those two were Mr. Greyson and his daughter. The trainer had no conception who it was that kept snapping an odd thousand to twenty or thousand to thirty about the horse, but he sent him sedulously along in his work, on the speculation that, whoever it might be, he would be sure to have a start for his money at all events, if only for hedging purposes. He did not in the least imagine it was the public. An uncertain-tempered brute like the Dancing Master was not at all the kind of animal that commends itself to the noble army of backers. Mr. Bill Greyson thought it much more likely that a syndicate of bookmakers had plotted to make a good thing out of the horse by working him in the betting-market like any other "corner" on the Stock Exchange, and in that case they would sooner or later inevitably have to make terms with him. He did not in the least believe that money was to be won by backing the grey, but he did think that he was the sort of horse that men skilful in the manipulation of the betting-market might frighten the public into rushing on at the last. He confided none of these imaginings to either his wife or daughter, but adhered faithfully to a pet maxim of his own, for which Bill Greyson had often been laughed at by his brother craftmasters: "Say nothing, but send 'em along."

Dollie, on the contrary, watched the

Cambridgeshire betting with the keenest interest. Gerald had told her nothing further about his plans, but she felt sure that it was on his behalf that the money was being so cautiously dribbled on to the Dancing Master. Always an early riser, she resumed an old habit rather laid aside of late years—the cantering up with her father in the early morning to see the horses at their work, and her heart swelled as she saw the strong resolute fashion in which the grey, when in the humour, galloped over his companions. She felt sure that if he liked he could, in racing parlance, make Caterham, Phaeton, and all the rest, "lie down," and she begged her father again and again to let her give the Dancing Master a gallop. Bill Greyson had seen what his daughter could do with a fractious colt many a time. There wasn't a lad about the place who didn't look upon Miss Dollie as a wonder in the saddle, while as for Joe Butters, he firmly believed Miss Dollie could do more with a bad-tempered colt than any jockey at Newmarket, but the trainer was not to be cajoled. He regarded the Dancing Master as really about the worst-tempered horse it had ever been his ill-luck to deal with, and he had no idea of permitting his only child to risk her bones on the back of the unmannerly brute.

But it so chanced business called Mr. Greyson away for a couple of nights, and he was consequently compelled to hand over his charges to the superintendence of Joe Butters, his very steady and capable lieutenant, and now came Dollie's opportunity. From her childhood she had domineered over Butters, who simply regarded her as a phenomenon. He thought there was nobody like her, that there was nothing she couldn't do if she tried, but he did rather demur when she told him the day after her father's departure that she would give the Dancer his gallop that morning. It was not for one moment that he doubted her ability to do so; if a horse could be ridden at all of course Miss Dollie could ride it; but he had a shrewd idea that old Greyson had forbidden this thing, and he knew that the stern old trainer was little likely to overlook any infraction of orders. Butters was too rigid a disciplinarian to dream of deviating from ordinary routine or the few commands left for his guidance, but Greyson had never thought it worth while to place a prohibition upon his daughter's whim

Joe, in short, was taken desperately aback at Dollie's request, and at last parried it with "Oh, I say Miss Dollie, you know he don't allow any one not duly insured to get upon that horse. Bless you, Miss, we keep him chiefly to work off the useless stable boys with. If you notice there's one missing every now and then. Well, we've put him on the

Dancer, and after a few minutes there's generally nothing left for us to do but pick up the pieces and cart 'em away for Christian burial."

"Yes, Joe, I know," rejoined Dollie, with preternatural gravity, although her eyes were dancing with fun, "but what I don't know, and must and will know, is where you do bury them?"

"It's a profound secret, and you'll never tell, promise?" replied Butters with a conscious twinkle in his eye. "We put 'em away at the back of the furzes, but you know, Miss Dollie, there'd be an awful row if we had to carry you there. No, leave the Dancer alone. We all know you can ride anything, but he isn't a lady's horse, Miss Dollie, he isn't indeed."

"Don't be a fool, Joe. You've seen me ride a good many that the veriest horse-coper out would hesitate to describe as that. Tell them to bring the Dancer up here at once, and shift my saddle."

"What a horse-coper would say, or what a wilful woman will do," thought Mr. Butters, " are a couple of equivalent conundrums a deal beyond me, but there's one thing I can swear to, and that is giving Miss Dollie her own way is only a matter of time as far as I am concerned. They most on 'em gets round me, but she —— Here, bring the Dancer up here; slip off, Matthews, and shift these saddles. Miss Dollie is going to give him a gallop this morning. If she can't make him go we may turn him up. It's not likely any of *you* can."

The Dancing Master eyed Dollie's short grey habit with undoubted distrust; and, active as the girl was, and clever as Butters and his myrmidons were in the handling of thoroughbreds, it was some little trouble to place her on his back; but Dollie had unbounded pluck, and, muttering between her white little teeth, " Gerald rode the horse for my sake, and

I'll do as much for him," she promptly responded to Butters's "Now, Miss Dollie," and, taking advantage of a slight lull in the grey's vagaries, was dropped into the saddle light as a bird. For a moment "the Dancer" seemed stupified by her audacity, a precious moment promptly utilised by the girl in settling herself in her seat, and then, as if in answer to her cheery "let his head go," the horse gave two tremendous plunges, and shook his head angrily. But Dollie remained immovable, her hands just played upon the bit lightly as they might have done upon a piano, while she spoke to the offender in soothing tones of expostulation. The grey seemed to consider the case, shook his head once more angrily, gave a vicious lash out that would have been bad for any one within reach, and then jumped off up the gallop at a rattling pace. Infirmities of temper the horse had, no doubt, but he was not cursed with that equine vice, "a hard mouth," and if Dollie's hands were light, they had little wrists strong as steel behind them. Before they had gone half-a-mile she felt that she had "the Dancer" well under control; and then the girl, with flushed face and sparkling eyes, took a steady pull at him, and sent him soberly along at three-quarter speed, talking to and encouraging him all the while, and, when in the last quarter of a mile she shook him up and finished at racing speed, the horse responded to her call, and ran home strong as a lion.

A perfect ovation from Butters and the stable-boys met Dollie as she pulled up. They had hold of the Dancer's head, and Butters jumped the girl off his back as quickly as possible.

"That's the best gallop he's done since we got him back from Newmarket, Miss Dollie," exclaimed that worthy, inexpressibly relieved to find that no harm had come of the girl's freak. "I never saw him go better."

"Go better, Joe! he's the sweetest galloper I was ever on. Smooth and easy as an express train; and what a stride! I don't believe we ever had such a horse at Riddleton before. Temper!—he's not a bad-tempered one. I'll tell you the secret of the Dancer: he has a very delicate mouth. In any other hands but mine that bit and bridoon would madden him. I'll ride him his gallops in future. Don't look frightened, Joe; but tell some one to bring up my hack. I'll make it all right with my father to-night."

And then Dollie rode home to breakfast with a strong conviction that she had done a good morning's work, and had something to tell her lover worth his knowing, if it was for him that the Dancer was so quietly but persistently backed for the Cambridgeshire.

The girl had every reason to be pleased with her prospects. She had stayed on in York for a fortnight or so after Gerald had left it, and during that time had seen a great deal of her future mother and sister-in-law, and to her great delight had got on wonderfully well with them. She owed this in some measure to herself, but she was quite aware that she was also indebted considerably to the fearless, outspoken Rector of St. Margaret's. John Thorndyke had been much taken with the girl. That he should study closely one about to be nearly connected with himself was only natural, and he was much pleased not only to find her so well educated and lady-like, but to discover that she possessed a large fund of practical common sense besides. Thorndyke stood up for the girl; he argued that Gerald might have done much worse; that we were fast merging into a democracy; and that the distinctions of rank would soon be things of the past; that she was a good, sensible, lady-like young woman, and would probably be an excellent wife to Gerald; and "that," added the Rector, "counts for much in a man's career."

That John Thorndyke's opinions were likely to carry much weight in St. Leonard's Place we know well, and the consequence was both Mrs. Rockingham and Ellen viewed the girl, so to speak, through John Thorndyke's spectacles, and made much of Dollie accordingly.

"Let us only win this big stake over the Cambridgeshire, and Gerald, my dear, I'll have the Dancer completely sobered down before you want him," said Dollie to herself; "and save Cranley—No, I'm afraid we can't do that—it's gone—but your people will welcome me cordially amongst them all the same," and with these somewhat incoherent reflections Dollie finished her breakfast.

CHAPTER X.

STEALING A KISS.

WILLIAM GREYSON, when, on his return that evening he was informed by Dollie of her morning's feat, shook his head gravely, and vowed he would give Joe Butters a bit of his mind in the morning.

"Dash it," he growled, "there's neither man, woman, nor boy I can trust about the place. The idea, you monkey, of your wanting to get on the Dancer. You knew I had forbidden it."

"Yes," said Dollie, demurely, "but you know when you tell a girl she mustn't she always feels she must."

"Ah, well, you've done it, and thank God no harm's come of it. But, if Joe Butters thinks I am going to stand such laxity about stable discipline as that, he's much mistaken."

"Now, father, listen to me," said Dollie. "You must not scold Butters, because I've bullied him since I was a child, and he didn't know how to say no to your daughter when she was peremptory. He was as frightened as you could have been till I was safely off the horse again. But mind, I'm going to ride the Dancer every morning, and you'll see he'll go quiet enough with me."

The trainer was at first emphatic in his denunciation of Butters, and scoffed at the idea of ever letting his daughter get on the horse again, but after a cigar and a jorum of hot grog he promised that Butters's offending should be condoned, and as for Dollie riding the Dancing Master again, well, he would see about it.

Bill Greyson was very proud and fond of his daughter, and as a horsewoman he believed there had never been her like. He had implicit confidence in her ability to ride anything, but he had hesitated about permitting her to try her hand on such a very queer-tempered brute as the Dancer. Now she had done it, and successfully too, and as he wended his way to bed the trainer turned it over in his mind, and thought there might not be much risk after all in letting the girl see to-morrow morning what she could make of him.

From this out Dollie rode the grey regularly in his morning work, and it was very singular how very much more tractable the horse became in her hands than he had hitherto been. It must not be supposed that he never showed temper; there was always trouble, for instance, about mounting. Custom did not seem to reconcile him to the habit skirt in the least, and he invariably entered an angry protest against its advent on his back. He would plunge and kick as of yore, and often require much coaxing to induce him to jump off on his gallop, but he unmistakably went much better when started than he had ever done with any one else. He rarely attempted to either bolt or stop when Dollie was sending him along, and, though Greyson deemed there was still little reliance to be placed upon him on a racecourse, the trainer certainly did think that the horse was improving.

The beginning of October found Cuthbert Elliston in all his glory. Every morning brought him a line from Riddleton to say that Caterham could not be doing better and there was every hope he would be as fit as hands could make him by the end of the month. The betting on the great handicaps was now getting heavy, and Elliston had already succeeded in backing his horse to win a very considerable stake. The public had left him the market very much to himself. Riddleton had the reputation amongst backers of being a very dangerous stable to meddle with, and though, in the first instance, they had nibbled a little at Caterham for the Cesarewitch it was not long before it oozed out that his owner had not got a shilling on him for that race, and that his starting was very doubtful. Then the public, disgusted at the apparently certain loss of their investments, vowed they would have no more of Mr. Elliston's horses, and hoped devoutly he might never win another race. The sporting public is a little apt to talk in that wise when it has burnt its fingers, but it soon forgets, and before long again follows the will-o'-the-wisp that has deceived it already.

It was just at this time when Cuthbert Elliston was positively revelling in "the possibility of the potentiality of riches," once more dreaming of having broken the Ring — that oft-recurring dream which never is realised—that he received a curt epistle from his partner which a little disconcerted him.

"Caterham is going like great guns," it said, " and on paper there's nothing to beat him, and, what is more, I feel sure that when we put him alongside our trying tackle he will quite confirm that opinion. I saw him last week, and he has never looked so well since he won the Two Thousand. But who's backing the Dancing Master ? Somebody undoubtedly keeps dribbling money on him if the Tattersall quotations can be trusted. Old Bill swears he knows nothing about it, for I asked him. However, the horse looks wonderfully well, and does his work, I am told, by himself. He is in the sale list, and Greyson has no intention, I believe, of even sending him to Newmarket, still, as I asked before, who is it persistently backs him?"

Elliston was not particularly put out by this letter, but he had been too long on the turf not to know, that, when meditating such a *coup* as he did, no chance that could be conceived was unworthy of consideration. He thought it would be as well, perhaps, if he ran up to York, had a look at Caterham, and explained to Greyson that he should not sanction his starting the Dancing Master for the Cambridgeshire; but before he started it would be as well perhaps to ascertain whose money it was that went so frequently on the Dancing Master. Upon applying to Broughton, with whom he had had many business transactions on the subject, the great north-country bookmaker replied, "I hardly know, sir. A little man named Johnson took all my book for both races before the weights were out, and he occasionally backs him again, but the horse is avowedly for sale, and, I should think, not likely to run for either, much less run straight if he does. But he's in your own stable, you know what his temper is."

"And who is this Johnson?" inquired Elliston, without paying any attention to ths latter part of Broughton's speech.

"Little man in a tall hat, sir. Bets chiefly on commission for a circle of small country clients, but I never knew him have the working of a *real* commission. His customers deal in fives and tens mostly. He's a straightforward little man enough, and I daresay he's parcelled out his Dancing Master money again before this."

All this was quite satisfactory to Elliston. He never dreamt of questioning the accuracy of the information because it chimed in exactly with his own view of the case, and in one sense the great

Northern bookmaker had told him the truth. Johnson and one or two of Johnson's colleagues were the backers of the Dancing Master, and it was perfectly true, as Broughton had said, that Johnson had taken the whole of his book upon both races about the horse at a very early period; but what Broughton did not tell Cuthbert Elliston was that he had an idea Johnson was this time cleverly working a very well authorised commission, and that he personally had taken more than one opportunity of what is termed "getting out," that is, backing the horse against which he had previously laid. In the first place, Broughton really did not know at whose inspiration Johnson was backing the Dancing Master, and, secondly, Cuthbert Elliston was a very unpopular man in the Ring. He was a hard man, who had punished them severely at times, and never given any of those whom he threatened to hit a hint to save themselves. As a rule the racing world generally rather chuckled when Cuddie Elliston was, to use their own expression, "warmed up," a feeling not at all confined to that section of the community, but prevalent amongst many little seaside *coteries*, who rejoice exceedingly when their neighbour is rumoured to have come to trouble over Egyptians or some similar popular delusion.

Mr. Elliston started for the North with a mind quite relieved as to the backers of the Dancing Master. He put it airily down to that great and long-suffering body, the British public, a public accustomed to pay dearly for its insufficient entertainment, accommodation, and its pastimes generally, and a public whose bounden duty it was, in Cuthbert Elliston's eyes, to lose money for the benefit of those who kept race-horses for their amusement. He did not pull up on this occasion at York, after his wont, and stay with his partner, but passed on straight to Riddleton, where he had telegraphed to Greyson to have something at the railway station to meet him. The trainer was there himself, and as they drove up to the Moor they naturally discussed the bearings of the Cambridgeshire together.

"The horse never was better," said Greyson, as they turned into the stable-yard. "I roughed him up this morning long before I got your telegram. Not quite a regular trial, but what we call a 'Yorkshire gallop,' and if, bar accident, you don't win the Cambridgeshire, I can only say there's a clipper in the background whose measure we've not got."

"No, I think it's good enough. Of course, you stand anything up to a hundred you like, taking the average of the commission," replied Elliston, "and the price is pretty good. I should like to see the horse at once," he continued.

as he stepped out of the trap, "and then you shall give me some lunch."

"All right, sir," said Greyson, "and I never showed you one with more pleasure. He's about fit to run now, but I know I can make him a bit better by the Houghton week."

The trainer might well look with pride into Elliston's face as the lad whipped the sheets off Caterham. He was as fine a specimen of a thoroughbred horse as ever was stripped. A rich, dark bay, standing at least sixteen one, and a rare good-looking horse. Old hypercritical turfites, rendered sceptical from losses over many a "beauty," would say, "Yes, that's just his weak point, he's a little too good-looking." I have heard infidels of this type talk in the same way about fashionable beauties, and pronounce them just a shade too handsome ever to mellow down for matrimony, and noticed as a fact that their plainer sisters have done better in that particular. Women, I suppose,

> Who, born for the universe, made up their mind
> Not a husband to give what was meant for mankind,

to paraphrase Goldsmith.

The Dancing Master was by no means so thoroughly handsome a horse, and yet his great ragged hips and low muscular thighs would have struck any judge of a racehorse, but then that little infirmity of a temper of his was well known, and no matter what his galloping points, or even capabilities, might be, that alone, amidst the crowds of people and the large fields of horses prevalent on English racecourses, was quite sufficient to forbid his being taken into much consideration. But Caterham was every inch a good-looking one. You could pick very few holes in the dashing winner of the Two Thousand, who, it was well known, had never been quite right or intended to win ever since.

The public had great and reasonable doubts of his soundness, and also thoroughly well justified grounds for mistrusting his owners' intentions, but the horse, as Elliston, no mean judge, admitted at once, had never looked better. His coat shone like burnished copper, and his eye looked clear, bright, and full as the evening star.

"He does you credit, Greyson, and if we are beat it won't be your fault. We've, partly from luck and partly from our clever tactics, thoroughly blinded the handicappers; they've given Phaeton 7lb. more than Caterham, and it should just be the other way I consider."

"Yes, sir, I should think this one could give Phaeton quite 7lb.; there was something like that between them this morning."

"It's good enough, bar accidents, and I have secured a very good jockey. Now, what about that grey of yours? Somebody's backing him, and he might be dangerous if he did take it into his head."

"Well, sir, it's no money of mine that goes on him, nor any belief of mine that he will ever win another race. He's in the sale list, and unless somebody buys him he won't even go to Newmarket."

"I needn't bother my head, then, any more about him," rejoined Elliston; "but come in and give me some lunch now. I'm in a hurry to get back to town."

The trainer quickly led the way back to the quaint, old-fashioned dining-room on the ground floor, with its low windows looking out on the grass-plot and the wide-spreading chestnut tree that decked its centre. The windows were half-open, letting in the scent of the creepers that covered the house and the flowers that still lingered in the borders surrounding it, for it was one of those soft autumns which made men loth to leave their summer haunts and return to the busy hum of cities.

Hap what may, there's never lack of provender for either man or horse about a racing establishment, and Elliston, who was rather given to the pleasures of the table, washed down an excellent meal with a flask of dry champagne, and then proceeded to aid its digestion with the help of a Cabana and some curious old brown sherry, much in repute amongst the frequenters of Riddleton.

"You gallop that bad-tempered brute of yours by himself, Greyson, I hear?" remarked Elliston, as he leant back in his chair in lazy enjoyment of his cigar.

"Yes, sir; and, to tell you the truth, Dollie usually rides him."

"What! You don't mean to tell me you've put the girl on a devil like that? Begad, if anything happens to her, hanging's too good for you."

"She got on him first without my

knowledge or consent. But she can do more with him now than any boy in the stable."

At this juncture a smart servant-girl entered the room, and, with a smile handing Greyson a note, intimated that the bearer was waiting.

The trainer glanced over it, and then, crushing it in his hand, said:

"I must ask you to excuse me, Mr. Elliston, a few minutes. The wife's away at York, but Dollie will give you your coffee, and tell you anything you want to know about 'The Dancer.'"

"All right! Mind I'm not late for my train," rejoined Elliston, who, having transacted his business and enjoyed his luncheon like the Sybarite he was, reflected that Dollie would be far pleasanter to talk to over his cigar than her father.

A minute or two later, and followed by a servant, bearing a tray with all the apparatus of coffee, Miss Dollie entered.

"God bless my soul, what a pretty girl you have grown!" exclaimed Elliston, honestly surprised to see how the girl's beauty had ripened within the last few months. "Upon my word, my dear, we must see about finding a husband for you."

"You're very good, Mr. Elliston," replied Dollie, with a coquettish toss of her head, "but pray don't trouble yourself."

"Ah! you think you can manage that for yourself, eh?" replied Elliston, laughing.

"I don't think it will be necessary to call in assistance, at all events. Will you take sugar?"

"No, thank you. But what have you been doing to yourself, child, to make yourself so much handsomer?"

"Riddleton air and morning gallops, I suppose," replied the girl; "but I flattered myself I wasn't so much amiss before."

"No more you were, Dollie," said Elliston, as he threw away the end of his cigar, and rose from his chair. "You've got lovely hair, child," and as he spoke he passed his hand caressingly over it.

"Don't, please, Mr. Elliston," cried the girl, instinctively shrinking back, and glancing up at his flushed face with dismay.

"Pooh, Dollie, you little prude! I've stroked your hair many a time as a child, when it wasn't so well worth stroking as it is now, and kissed you too, my dear, when you were not quite so well worth kissing as you are now," and as he spoke Elliston suddenly passed his arm round the girl's waist, and pressed his sherry-stained lips to hers.

Dollie gave a half cry, and tried fiercely to thrust back the aggressor, but he was too strong for her, and, holding her fast in his arms, repeated the offence with the brutal taunt, "Bah, you little idiot, your mother would never have made so much fuss about such a trifle."

As he spoke the sash of the window was thrown quite up. A slight figure sprang through it, and as Elliston turned to confront the new comer he received a straight left-hander in the chest that sent him back reeling.

"Oh, Gerald, Gerald, what have you done? Oh, please, please," cried Dollie, bursting into tears.

"Done!" exclaimed Gerald, in tones hoarse with passion, "done my best to knock down the biggest blackguard in England."

Elliston recovered himself with a mighty effort. His eyes gleamed with fury, and in a low grating voice he said, "You young scoundrel; you shall pay for this," and gathering himself together was about to rush on his antagonist.

But quick as thought Gerald passed Dollie behind him, and, throwing himself into fighting attitude, coolly awaited the rush of his cousin. Despite his superior size, height, and it may be presumed strength, Elliston suddenly realised that Gerald's chastisement was not a thing to be lightly accomplished. He saw at a glance that Gerald could use his hands. Thrashing him off-hand was one thing, but a stand-up fight was rather too undignified a proceeding at his age. Mastering his rage with a mighty effort, he exclaimed with a bitter sneer, " I congratulate you upon having so thoroughly acquired the habits of the class to which you belong, but gentlemen don't settle their differences in that fashion. Adieu, Miss Dollie. I dare say Forrest will find you by no means so coy with your kisses."

Gerald started, and was about to rush upon his cousin, but Dollie's hand upon his arm restrained him. He made no further answer than a contemptuous smile, while Elliston, after one glance to gauge the effects of his Parthian dart, stalked angrily from the room.

CHAPTER XI.

GOING FOR THE GLOVES.

ELLISTON left the house in search of the trap that was to convey him to the station literally swelling with indignation. This whelp of a boy seemed to confront him at every turn, and, what was worse, to checkmate him. From winning a big stake to the buying of Cranley, or snatching a kiss from Dollie Greyson, Gerald was always in his way. He felt there was nothing he would shrink from to work woe to his cousin, but Gerald was under the wing of Lord Whitby, and had achieved a position besides of his own that made him tolerably unassailable.

Still, as be bade the trainer good-bye, he bethought him of a thorn to plant in Gerald's breast.

"Good-bye, Greyson," he said, "we shall win the Cambridgeshire, never fear, and winter in clover; but I've got one hint to give you. I see that young Rockingham is hanging round here after your daughter. That will do her no good. He was as wild as a hawk at college, and, like all his stock, is pretty unscrupulous with regard to women. A hint's enough to a man of your experience. Lock up your daughter, and hunt that young reprobate off the premises. You'll find him kissing her in the dining-room now, most likely," and before Greyson could reply Elliston jumped into the trap and was gone.

This was too much in accord with his own ideas not to make the trainer very uncomfortable. He did not even know that Gerald was at Riddleton, the note that summoned him from the dining-room relating only to the delivery of some forage. As he strolled back to the house across the grass-plot he mused rather grimly over the unfortunate entanglement of his daughter, and at last, happening to raise his eyes, saw through the open window the tableau Elliston had so deftly painted to him. There was Gerald in most lover-like attitude with his arm round Dollie's waist, and unmistakeably kissing her.

This was too much for Greyson's equanimity. He dashed into the house, and entered the dining-room abruptly. Dollie made an attempt to extricate herself from her lover's embrace on seeing him, but Gerald held her fast.

"Mr. Rockingham," said the trainer, "I'll have none of this. I told you so as Jim Forrest, and I tell you so much more strongly now I know who you are. I'll not have my girl's head turned with your nonsense. She may be but a giddy little simpleton, but she is my daughter, and all I have got."

"Oh, father, hear me," cried Dollie, for there was a touch of pathos in the hard old man's voice that went to her heart. "No, let me go to him, Gerald," but her lover still held her tight.

"Go to your room at once," rejoined Greyson, "and you, sir, don't attempt to detain her. I will send you to the station, but never let me catch you on Riddleton Moor again."

Dollie at last twisted herself out of her lover's embrace, and was about to rush across to her father when Gerald caught her wrist and exclaimed, "Stay. Mr. Greyson, there's no harm in kissing the girl you are pledged to marry. I have promised to take Dollie for my wife if you will give her to me."

"Mighty pretty words," rejoined the trainer roughly, "such as young gentlemen of your class think it no harm to pour into the ears of foolish girls beneath them. Do you suppose for one instant that your own people would allow you to make such a marriage as that?"

"I know in a few months I shall be of age, and that nobody will be able to prevent me. Besides, Dollie will tell you that she has already been welcomed as my future wife by my mother and sister."

"It's true, father, it is indeed; they were most kind."

"And do you mean to tell me that they knew that Dollie was the daughter of Bill Greyson, the trainer?"

"Certainly, I do," replied Gerald; "just as much as they know that I am Jim Forrest, the jockey."

For a minute or two Greyson stood silently glancing from one to the other of them. He could not quite take in the reality of the situation. It seemed to him almost absurd to talk of a Rockingham marrying a daughter of his; and yet, surely, if there were nothing in it, Mrs. Rockingham would hardly have welcomed Dollie, as the girl declared she had. Pooh! they were young in the ways of the world; and because Mrs. Rockingham had been good-natured and kind to his little girl, and perhaps smiled at their philandering, they had both jumped to the conclusion that she would be pleased to receive her as a daughter-in-law. And then Elliston's parting admonition recurred to him. Yes; that was much more likely that young Rockingham was just amusing himself with a flirtation.

"Mr. Greyson, will you give me Dollie?" said Gerald after some length, and still holding the girl's hand.

"I think not. I'll take some little time to consider; but I don't believe any good would come of such a marriage. Mr. Elliston warned me just before he started against letting you make a fool of my girl."

"Cuthbert Elliston!" exclaimed Gerald "the scoundrel!—what has he to do with it?"

"He's one of your family anyhow. It was he told me you were here, and that I should find you both billing and cooing in the parlour."

"And did he tell you that I nearly knocked him down for his impudent behaviour to your daughter?" interposed Gerald, hotly.

"What!" exclaimed Greyson, sharply.

"Indeed," said Dollie; "Mr. Elliston was very rude to me, and I was very glad when Gerald jumped in at the window."

"I only know," said Gerald, "I found my precious cousin—who has a wife of his own, remember—making the most violent love to Dolly, very much to her annoyance; and that I did my best to knock him down—and all but succeeded."

"Ah! you struck him?" said Greyson

between his set teeth; "that was well done," he added after a pause.

"And now, Mr. Greyson, will you give me Dollie?" said Gerald.

"Go to your room, girl; and leave Mr. Rockingham and me to talk matters over. You needn't be afraid, child; we're not going to quarrel."

Dollie made no reply; but, with a bright smile at her lover, tripped out of the dining-room.

"Now, Greyson," said Gerald, "I have come here for a good long talk with you about more things than one. First, I am in thorough earnest about wishing to marry your daughter. I have taken her to see my mother and sister; they both like her, and will be very glad to welcome her into the family, of which, remember, I am now the head. As for my rascally cousin, he ruined my father, and would do the same by me if he could. He has nothing to do with our concerns further than to pay us some, at all events, of what he owes us. I can't marry Dollie yet for some months, at all events; I think it best to stick to my profession closely for a little longer, so you will have time to consider the subject. That's finished for the present. Of course we shall correspond; it's no use your saying we shan't, because in these days that never prevents young people, who are fond of one another, doing it—promotes duplicity, nothing more. Now, is the Dancer still yours?"

"Yes, worse luck; and likely to continue so. I had hopes when I saw they were backing him a bit for the Cambridgeshire that somebody might be disposed to make a bid of some sort; but nobody speaks."

"And he's quite well?"

"Well. Of course he is. Ask Dollie, she gallops him every morning. The beggar never looked better."

"You don't mean to say you put her

up on that queer-tempered animal?" exclaimed Gerald.

"No," replied Greyson, "but she took advantage of my absence to put herself up; and there's no nonsense about it, he goes better with her than he ever did with any one, not barring yourself, Mr. Rockingham."

"Good! Now, Greyson, the Cambridgeshire betting about the Dancing Master, as far as it has gone, represents pretty well my commission. Somebody, of course, has been clever enough to risk a little about the thing on spec, with the haziest intentions as to what he was speculating in. Some one always does. But I have got on the Dancer to win a rattling stake as it is, and, if I find him what I hope, can easily get a good bit more at a longish price. You mean to run him, of course. With seven stone twelve the race is a gift to him if he chooses."

"Just so, *if he chooses*, but he never does choose. No, he's not worth sending to Newmarket, Mr. Rockingham; and what's more, we've got another here we think quite good enough to serve our turn."

"Yes, I know. Cuthbert has backed Caterham to win him a lot of money, but my impression is that the Dancer is a tremendous horse when he runs kind. He'd beat Caterham far enough at even weights, though the latter's a good horse, too. You've not promised he shan't go to Newmarket, have you?"

"No, certainly not. I told Mr. Elliston I had no intention of sending him there; but he knows the horse is for sale, and if any one buys him I can't be answerable for what his new owner may think fit to do."

"But still he's your horse. You're quite within your right in beating Mr.

Elliston, if you can, for a good stake like the Cambridgeshire."

"I tell you, sir, he's no good. With his temper, he'd never try in a big field such as there will be for that race."

"Recollect," replied Gerald, impressively, "the only time the Dancer ever won I rode him. Recollect how he recognised my voice the other day in the stable. I don't pretend my riding had anything to do with his winning, but simply the horse knew me, and did for me what he has done for nobody else."

"There may be something in that," rejoined the trainer, musingly, "but hang it, I don't like interfering with stable tactics."

"Then," said Gerald, "I ask you to choose between my interests and Cuthbert Elliston's, between the interests of the man who insulted your daughter and the interests of the man who hopes to marry —— "

Greyson started as if stung.

"Yes," he rejoined, in stern, resolute tones, "that settles it. If I can beat him fairly for the Cambridgeshire, by —— I will. Mr. Rockingham, play your game as you like. You can depend upon me, bar accidents, to hand you over the Dancing Master when the saddling-bell rings as fit as hands can make him, with no other orders than win if you can. There's my hand, sir."

The two exchanged hand-grips, and then the trainer said:

"Tell me it's not flying in the face of your own people, and will do you no harm with them, and, after the Cambridgeshire, if you ask me for Dollie again, Mr. Rockingham, I'll give her you, win or lose."

"That's a bargain, Mr. Greyson," said Gerald, as they once more shook hands.

"And now I'll send Dollie to you. She can tell you more about the Dancer than

I can, but I do believe this, that he's a good deal better than Caterham *if* he will try," and with this dubious assurance the trainer left the room.

Dollie was not very far off, and reappeared speedily at her father's summons.

"It's all right, darling," cried Gerald, joyously, as he clasped the girl in his arms and kissed her. "Your father's behaved like a trump. I'm to marry you after the Cambridgeshire; and the Dancer's to win it; and I'm going to land money enough to buy back Cranley Chase. I'm pretty sure Whitby don't really want it, and would let *me* have it for what he gave for it. I'm a great favourite with the old lord."

"Oh, Gerald! if you could! How proud I should feel then that it was at my recommendation you turned jockey!"

"You may feel proud of that as it is, sweet," replied her lover; "but your father tells me you've been riding the

Dancer, and that he goes tolerably quiet with you."

"Yes: he kicks and plunges, of course, and he sulks a bit with me at starting; but he goes very well with me when we are fairly off; and, Gerald, I never was on the back of such a galloper!"

"Do you find him pull much?"

"No; and that's been the mistake with him all along. He has a rather delicate mouth, and likes to have his head. If you pull at him with that heavy bit and bridoon bridle they put on him he gets mad, and then you know neither man nor horse ever feels pain. I have gone on riding him in that way, but then you know how light a woman's hand is. Gerald, dear, take my advice, and put a plain snaffle on him for the Cambridgeshire."

"I daresay you're right, Dollie. Your father, though he hadn't quite mastered the theory, had always an inkling of it.

'Leave him alone,' were his orders before the Two Thousand; 'he may win the race himself, but you won't make him.' As a stable-boy, I rode him strictly according to orders, only too anxious no fault should be found with me in that respect; as a jockey, I might have had ideas of my own on the subject, and, hard as I always try to carry out my employer's instructions, there are times when to stick to them seems to be throwing the race away, and sometimes actually is. Neither owner, trainer, nor any one else can foresee the turns-up in a race, nor the way in which it will be run. It may be run all false, and a clever jockey, who knows his business, sees his one chance is to throw all orders to the wind and rely on his own judgment. You are told to wait, but know amongst your antagonists there's one with a terrible turn of speed, and there's nothing will make the running. Your only chance is to do it yourself, and stand the abuse if you're unsuccessful. But forgive me, Dollie; I am delivering quite a sermon on my own profession; it's a profession I love, and can't help getting a little enthusiastic about."

"And do you think I'm not proud of the name you've made in it? I believe I think more of Jim Forrest, if possible, than Gerald Rockingham."

"And Gerald's not jealous of Jim," replied her lover, laughing. "And now, dearest, it's time I was off; but mind, Dollie, you must be there to see me win the Cambridgeshire. Tell your father it must be so. I shan't see you again till we meet at Newmarket, and then, hey! for winning the last big handicap of the season and Cranley Chase."

"Here's the Cambridgeshire and Cranley Chase!" cried Dollie, snatching a wine-glass from the luncheon-table and waving it over her head. "*Vive la guerre!* and success to the sky-blue and white."

"Good-bye, dearest," said Gerald, as he once more clasped his *fiancée* in his arms; "and God grant your toast may prove true. Take care of the Dancer for me; and mind you are there in the Houghton week."

One more kiss, and Gerald Rockingham was gone, and Dollie, dropping into a chair, was soon lost in the sweetest of dreamy reveries.

CHAPTER XII.

AT THE RUTLAND ARMS.

The Monday of the Houghton Meeting has come at last, and the week gives promise of capital sport. Never had the betting on the Cambridgeshire been heavier, and never perhaps had the early backers experienced more discomfitures. Favourite after favourite was sent to the right about, either from having failed to stand a preparation, or in consequence of owners finding themselves so forestalled by the rapacity of the public that it was impossible to obtain a fair and reasonable price about their horses. This naturally gave fresh courage to the bookmakers, and the big handicap could boast now of a very elastic market.

The principal feature on the Heath on Monday between the intervals of racing was a strong desire to back the Dancing Master, a thing that astonished Messrs. Elliston and Pearson not a little. They could not make out exactly who was doing it. Mr. Johnson, no doubt, was picking up the long odds at every favourable opportunity, but there were more Richmonds in the field than one, and before the racing finished and the crowd flocked back to spruce little Newmarket, the Dancing Master had been brought from the forty-to-one division to something like over half the price. All sorts of rumours were current about him. It was reported that there had been a great trial at Riddleton, and that Caterham, one of the prominent favourites, had been well beaten by his stable companion. That the horse was not known to have arrived was nothing. Bill Greyson and his string were not expected till the afternoon, and it was quite likely might not arrive till the next day, the Cambridgeshire being set for Wednesday's card. Ere they reached the Rutland, Elliston and his partner had learnt, upon unimpeachable authority, that Greyson had arrived, and brought the Dancing Master with him as well as Caterham.

Over their dinner that evening the two indulged in various conjectures as to the meaning of this freak of old Bill's. The most probable solution in their eyes was that he had sold the horse, and that his new owner had thrown the commission into the market. Well, they agreed it was not likely to signify much

"Some new young one anxious to distinguish himself by winning a big race first time of asking," said Elliston. "He's likely to pay dearly for his whistle; what with the money the Ring take out of him over it, and the price old Greyson has probably put that worthless brute into him at, if he don't have an expensive race on Wednesday I'm much mistaken."

"Greyson, of course, will be up to see us about breakfast time to-morrow. It's no use speculating about who he's made a fool of over the Dancing Master; let's go down to the Rooms and see what's doing."

"All right!" replied Elliston, as he lit a fresh cigar, "come along."

Business at the Rooms was in a languid state when the parties left them. A good many of the leading bookmakers were there discussing the events of the day, but none of the leading dons of the racing world had as yet put in an appearance. The former were apparently no little exercised in their minds about the mysterious apparition of the Dancing Master in the betting-market. It was now known that the horse had arrived, but in whose interest he was running, and who was to ride him, were matters that seemed to trouble the minds of the leading magnates of the ring no little. Elliston was at once hailed with proffers of odds against the Dancing Master, but the refusal of both himself and Pearson to invest on his chance seemed once more to puzzle the very suspicious members of Tattersall's— sensitive ever from long experience to dynamite mines of this nature exploded upon them at the last moment. True, he had shown himself thoroughly unreliable on account of temper for at least two years, but he had proved himself, and very unexpectedly too, a great horse upon one occasion, and the brethren of the mystic circle are bound to keep such facts within their memories, or break.

But soon after ten Sir Marmaduke, accompanied by Farrington and two other of his friends, strolled in, and the listlessness that had rather characterised the proceedings was put aside. So far there had been very little business doing, nothing except desultory talk had been the outcome of the evening. But the baronet had startled the Ring too often not to make his advent a matter of interest. They knew very well that he had experienced a most disastrous year, and that his own stable was under one of those periodical blights that such establishments suffer from. But Sir Marmaduke was rather catholic in his taste for speculation, and by no means confined his operations to backing his own horses. Heavy loser though he undoubtedly was on the season, yet he had enjoyed gleams of sunshine, and had made the very Ring open its eyes with the daring plunges he had made on some of Lord Whitby's "good things." When he laid five to one in thousands *on* a colt of that nobleman's for the New Stakes at Ascot, the racing world marvelled; but when he followed it up by betting seven thousand to four *on* the winner of the Gold Cup, the old hands shook their heads, and said that, though in these two instances fortune had favoured him, yet a Nemesis would surely overtake one who wooed the fickle goddess so rashly.

"Dancing Master for the Cambridgeshire?" he said quietly to one of the boldest of the bookmaking fraternity.

"Twenty to one, Sir Marmaduke. Do you want it to money?" was the reply.

"I'll take it in thousands," rejoined the baronet.

"Can't do it, Sir Marmaduke. I haven't so much money left to lay. Shall I put down twenty monkeys? Ten thousand to five hundred is a nice bet."

The baronet nodded, and almost immediately afterwards the languid voice of Captain Farrington was heard inquiring after the Dancing Master, and he, too, was accommodated upon similar terms.

It was speedily apparent that the little coterie of whom Sir Marmaduke was the guiding star were all intent on backing this horse, and the odds shortened rapidly. Still the fielders continued to lay the lessening price. They recalled how these very men had put faith in the Dancing Master at Ascot, and how he had proved but a broken reed to them then. However, sheer weight of money tells in the betting-ring just as it does on the Stock Exchange, and "the bulls" upon this occasion brought the Dancing Master to ten to one taken freely before they closed the operations.

"What do you think of all this?" said Pearson, as the pair strolled home to the Rutland.

"Think?" answered Elliston, irritably; "I think that Sir Marmaduke means to have another shy with the Dancing Master; that though he sent him back to Riddleton he never gave up his control of the horse, and that all Bill Greyson's story about his being in the sale-list was gammon, or at all events premature. I shall give that old villain a pretty stiff corner of my mind to-morrow."

"I wonder who rides?" said Pearson.

"Oh! Blackton, no doubt. He's Sir Marmaduke's first jockey, and will probably declare three or four pounds over weight. But he didn't do much with the horse in the Hunt Cup."

"No," said Pearson, as he rang for a brandy and seltzer, that peaceful haven, the Rutland, being at length attained, "but I've an unpleasant presentiment that cursed grey will trouble us somehow in the big race on Wednesday. He'll knock our horse down, or run away from the lot, as he did in the Guineas two years ago. By the way, I hope young Rockingham won't have the mount."

"No fear. He quarrelled with Sir Marmaduke about something, and hasn't worn his colours the last year or more. Just the young beggar's luck. He got Whitby's riding instead. Left the sinking ship just in time to join another that had both royals and stunsails set."

"And the lad knows how to follow his luck," said Pearson, moodily. "If by any fluke that boy's on the Dancing Master I shall cover my money by backing him for a little."

"You always did funk," sneered Elliston; "but I don't think, unless the horse is, as I guess, still Sir Marmaduke's, old Greyson will send him to the post after all."

"He will," rejoined Pearson. "He daren't bring him to Newmarket and not run him. Now I'm off to bed. Goodnight."

The attorney was up and out on the Heath betimes to see and hear what was doing, and astonished his partner on his return not a little with the intelligence that Jim Forrest was to ride the Dancing Master.

"At least, that's what I heard this morning, and everybody's puzzled to know who's pulling the strings. He was out this morning and looked fit as fiddles, but showed a deal of temper till Forrest got on him. He did a nice canter with him, and went fairly kind. Greyson's coming up to see us about ten."

"And Caterham?"

"Went a good strong gallop, and looks fit to run for a kingdom. Greyson says he never was better."

They were still dawdling over their cigars and the card of the day, when the trainer was announced, and at once proceeded to give due account of his charges, all of whom he pronounced emphatically thoroughly fit to meet their engagements, especially the Cambridgeshire crack, Caterham. "Though," he added, "they tell me, in consequence of what took place at the Rooms last night, that old grey of mine looks like passing him in the betting."

"Oh, I want to speak to you about that," said Elliston, sharply. "Has Sir Marmaduke anything to do with the horse now?"

"Nothing whatever, sir."

"Then what the devil did you send that satanic-tempered brute here for, after telling me you didn't intend to?"

"I changed my mind. My horse happens to be very well, and I don't see why I shouldn't have a cut in for a stake worth over two thousand," replied Greyson, doggedly. "You've no call to complain about Caterham, he's just about as fit as I know how to make him. It's not very likely the Dancer *will* beat you, but I warn you he can *if he likes.*"

"And pray may I ask whether it is from your inspiration that Sir Marmaduke and his friends are plunging on the Dancer in this manner?"

"No, sir, I honestly don't know what has induced Sir Marmaduke and his friends to back the horse in the way I hear they did last night. But it was from no hint of mine. He'll run, but I don't much believe in him."

"And suppose I tell you that I particularly wish that he should not run. What then?"

"I shall be sorry to disoblige you, Mr. Elliston, but I've brought him to Newmarket, and he'll run all the same," replied Greyson, quietly.

"A plant, by Heaven!" cried Elliston, fiercely. "My horse, I presume, has been sacrificed to yours."

"Nothing of the sort, sir," replied Greyson. "Yours is as well as ever he was in his life. The two have never been put together, and it's sheer guess-work on my part that the grey's the best."

"And is that young whelp, Forrest, to ride the Dancer?" snarled Elliston.

"Mr. Rockingham is to ride my horse. I don't know about his being a young whelp, or a young anything else," rejoined Greyson, pretty sharply. "I do know that he's about the best jockey of the day, and that if he gets well away, and the Dancer runs kind, he'll spreadeagle his field to-morrow."

"With those views we may say, I think, Pearson, that he trains no more for us?"

"No," said the attorney, with a malicious grin, "and, if the Dancing Master does win the Cambridgeshire, perhaps Mr. Greyson will have cause to wish he had yielded to wiser counsels."

"I've not forgotten that I'm your debtor, Mr. Pearson, but I'll take my chance. I daresay, if it comes to the worst, I shall find friends to assist me in meeting my liabilities. Good morning, gentlemen."

"A case of mutiny, by Jove!" exclaimed Elliston, as the door closed behind the trainer.

"It's your own fault in great measure," said Pearson, savagely. "If you hadn't given Greyson that cursed grey colt we should have been masters of the situation."

"And intend to be so still. But do you honestly think there's a chance of the Dancing Master beating us?"

"Yes," replied Pearson, "I do. I wouldn't back the horse, he's so thoroughly uncertain; but I agree with Greyson, that he's a great horse when he likes, probably the best we ever had at Riddleton. It's an old axiom—never overlook an animal's best form. I never saw the Two Thousand easier won, and, remember, subsequent running showed that he had a good field behind him. I wish heartily that he wasn't going to start."

As he spoke the door opened softly, and Dollie, who was in search of her father, peeped in.

"We never had such a chance," continued the attorney, "and it would be too provoking, after having got on to win such a big stake so cleverly, to have the prize snatched from our grasp by that perverse-tempered brute. I can't imagine what has made Greyson so contumacious. There's something behind I don't understand."

Cuthbert Elliston did not think it necessary to enlighten his partner about that little *contretemps* up at Riddleton, though he had no doubt that his folly there had caused this combination against him. Dollie had no doubt told her father what had occurred, and Gerald had persuaded the trainer to repay the affront put on his daughter in this fashion.

"That blackguard young villain," he muttered, "planned this little scheme for my discomfiture."

"It don't much matter what's the cause, Sam," he said at last. " If Greyson won't take orders he must take the consequences. I'll take care the Dancing Master don't start. Listen to me," and he lowered his voice, so that Dollie could no longer catch what he was saying.

But the girl had heard quite enough. Closing the door noiselessly behind her, she sped down the passage like a lapwing, with a view to carrying this piece of intelligence as quickly to her lover as might be.

CHAPTER XIII.

GETTING AT THE FAVOURITE.

DOLLIE hurried away from the Rutland with Cuthbert Elliston's words ringing in her ears, " I'll take care the Dancing Master doesn't start," and she felt certain that he would, if possible, make good his word. She had caught but a fragment of their conversation, but it was quite enough to make her thoroughly understand the situation. It was evident from Pearson's speech that the two men hoped to win a very large stake over Caterham, and equally clear that they were afraid of the Dancing Master upsetting their plans, and were much disconcerted by his unexpected appearance at

Newmarket. She knew her father was to see them that morning—indeed, had expected to find him with them. From Elliston's words she thought it was pretty clear that he not only had seen them, but had refused to strike the Dancing Master out of the Cambridgeshire. "If Greyson won't take orders he must take consequences:" that surely could only mean that her father had declined to obey his patrons on this point, and Dollie was much too conversant with turf history not to know that when Elliston said he would take care the horse should not start foul play of some kind was contemplated.

Were all Gerald's hopes to be frustrated in this wise? No! Something must be done to prevent it! What villainy was meditated? She must see Gerald at once. He would know what was best to be done. It was clear there was no time to be lost; but where was she to find him? She did not know where he lodged, and it was getting time for the day's racing to commence. Once on the heath, he might be so engaged as to leave no opportunity for speaking with him the whole afternoon. And yet she felt sure that her news would brook no delay in the telling. At last she bethought herself of the stables where her father's charges were standing, and made her way thither.

The first person she encountered in the yard was Joe Butters, who, seated on an upturned stable bucket, was solacing himself with a tankard of mild ale and a little tobacco, previous to commencing his duties on the course.

"Where is Mr. Rockingham?" inquired Dollie. "I must speak with him at once, Joe! Do you think you could find him?"

"Well, miss," replied Butters, as he leisurely rose from his seat, "Mr. Rockingham cantered up to the heath about ten minutes ago. He said he had to see Lord Whitby before the racing began."

"But you are going up with the horses, Joe?"

"Yes, miss, in about half-an-hour. We've nothing in the first two races."

"Well, of course you'll see Mr. Rockingham."

"I don't know about to speak to. You see, Jim—I mean Mr. Rockingham—don't ride for us as a rule, though I do hear he's to ride the Dancer to-morrow. My word, Miss Dollie, but we ought to set the bells ringing at Riddleton this time. Why, if the Dancer only tries, our pair ought to finish first and second for the Cambridgeshire."

"And which do you like the best, Joe?" inquired the girl, eagerly.

"Well, I've got my pound on Caterham. You see he is a horse you can depend upon. If you was only going to ride the Dancer yourself, Miss Dollie, I fancy he would win far enough."

"Never mind that. You shall have a

pound on the Dancer with me. He ran straight enough with Mr. Rockingham before, Joe; and mind, he will again to-morrow. Now listen to what I've got to say to you. If you cannot see Mr. Rockingham yourself, you must manage to get this message sent to him: say that I wish to see him on a matter of the greatest importance as soon as possible."

"All right, miss; I'll manage it somehow. Mr. Rockingham will know where you are, I suppose?"

"Yes; he has only to ask father. Don't forget—of the greatest importance, remember." And, with an emphatic little nod, Dollie walked quickly away to prepare for the heath.

Mr. Greyson had chartered one of those mysterious ramshackle vehicles to convey Mrs. Greyson and Dollie to the heath which seems almost peculiar to Newmarket; though the racecourse fly has a family resemblance all over the country.

One peculiarity about them is that they occasionally have an equine celebrity, grievously fallen from his high estate, between the shafts. I remember seeing in a Stockbridge trap of this description a horse whose parents had both taken classic honours at Epsom: his sire had won the Derby, his mother the Oaks; and similar glories had been expected from him in his youth. And this, after all, was the termination of his career!

The racing proved, as is often the case at Newmarket on an off-day, of a very tame description; and Dollie awaited the advent of her lover with scarce-controlled impatience. The one feature of the afternoon's sport was when, in intervals between the races, the Cambridgeshire was introduced, a growing desire to back the Dancing Master was evident; and it was whispered about that a strong commission was in the market, although not apparently emanating from the stable. Ellis ton and his partner were more puzzled than ever at the aspect of affairs.

At length Gerald cantered up on his hack, and raised his hat amidst the admiring stare of the surrounding crowd; for the "gentleman jockey" was by this time not only well known but immensely popular. Quickly it was buzzed about that the ladies "Jim Forrest was a-talking to" were the wife and daughter of Bill Greyson, who owned the now first favourite for the Cambridgeshire; for Lord Whitby's heavy commission, on the top of the big investments of Sir Marmaduke and his friends, had at length placed the Dancing Master at the head of the poll; and it was by this time no secret that "the gentleman jockey," as his admirers delighted to call him, would ride that erratic animal.

"Ten thousand pardons, Dollie, dearest; but I only got your message an hour or so ago, and am so busy I couldn't get here before. As it is I have had to bucket my hack unmercifully. Good-day, Mrs. Greyson, the sport is not of much account this afternoon, but, if we get the black and crimson home first to-morrow, it won't be a dull week, you know, altogether."

"And you will, won't you, Mr. Rockingham?"

"I hope so," he replied, laughing. "And now, Dollie," he continued, lowering his voice, "what is it? I've no time to lose, as I must get back to ride Grand Turk in the next race."

"There's something wrong about the Dancing Master, Gerald. I've overheard Cuthbert Elliston say that he would take care he didn't start."

"Ha!—who to?" inquired Rockingham, eagerly.

"To Mr. Pearson."

"And there was no one else present; and they don't know you overheard them?"

"There were only those two in the room, and I feel sure they don't know I was within earshot."

"This must be seen to as soon as possible. Both Elliston and Pearson are on the course, I have seen them. Meet me at the stables as soon as you can. I shall ride straight back after the next race, as I have no mount in the concluding one. I have proved a little too much for Cuthbert once or twice already, and I shouldn't wonder if I do again. Good-bye, Dollie, for the present. On you go, Captain Barclay," and Gerald just pressed his hack with his knees, and the docile brute swung into a hand-canter at once, and in obedience to his master's hand made his way to the starting-post for the Bretby Stakes Course."

Gerald called his hack after the famous pedestrain, saying he was always doing his 1,000 miles over the Heath after the manner of his godfather.

Dollie found little difficulty in persuading her mother to leave the course before the last race. It was the good lady's first visit to Newmarket, and to tell the truth she was not very favourably impressed with it. She found it dull. At York she had lots of friends and acquaintances to chat with, which to her was half the fun of a race-meeting. Then the perpetual change of course bothered her, and she came to the conclusion that they managed these things infinitely better in the North, so that she was quite willing to drive home to tea as soon as her daughter suggested it.

Her mother once comfortably deposited in their lodgings, Dollie immediately slipped down to the stables, where she found Gerald awaiting her, and at once told him her story.

Gerald listened very attentively, and when she had finished, said:

"There can be no doubt about it.

They have, I know, backed Caterham to win a very large stake, and the appearance of the Dancer on the scene has frightened them. Your father has most likely told them, if he chooses to run kind the grey will beat them, and also declined to scratch the horse. Elliston undoubtedly means foul play of some sort. I shall sleep in the stable, and watch the Dancer's box myself, to-night, and take care that either Butters or myself are with him till the Cambridgeshire's over. Now run home, and say nothing to any one of what you have overheard. Good-bye, dearest; I should have come up to spend the evening, but don't expect to see anything of me now till after the race.'

No sooner had Dollie disappeared than Gerald went in search of Butters. That worthy was speedily found in the immediate vicinity, discussing the race with some of his own class, and giving it as his opinion that one of the Riddleton pair would win. Further pressed upon the subject, he informed his hearers that he preferred Caterham himself, but that Mr. Forrest was the greatest horseman of the day, and, with the Dancing Master in his hands, there was no knowing what might happen.

Just as he delivered himself of this oracular opinion, the gentleman jockey himself appeared, and was immediately an object of great attraction to the little knot of stablemen to whom Mr. Butters had been holding forth.

"Here, Joe, I want you," exclaimed Gerald.

"All right, Mr. Rockingham. What is it?" replied Butters, not a little gratified to show the intimate terms he was on with the great man to the little circle he was leaving. A bit of snobism common to people of infinitely higher station than Joe Butters.

"I want to see the horses at once, Joe. Have you got the key of the stable?"

"I've one, and Mr. Greyson another," replied Butters, as he led the way thither without further comment.

They entered the stable, which consisted of four loose boxes and a couple of roomy stalls. One of these latter contained a considerable amount of clean straw. The other was empty save for a large corn-bin which stood in its entrance. The boxes were all tenanted by Greyson's charges.

"This is the Dancer's box, isn't it?" said Gerald, as he walked towards the one at the far end from the door.

"Yes; and Caterham's next him."

Gerald opened the box and went in. The horse looked round, and gave a low whinny of recognition. He was evidently in the very bloom of condition—his coat shone like satin, and his eye, clear and bright, denoted that the animal was in perfect health. Gerald cast a keen glance at the horse's legs, and saw they were clean and flat, such as gladden the heart of a trainer. He walked up to the Dancer and examined him closely. He was apparently satisfied with the result of his examination, for as he closed the box-door behind him he muttered, "All's safe so far."

"Now, Joe," he continued aloud, "what you and I have got to do is this—One or other of us must never leave the horse till after to-morrow's race. I've just heard, on good authority, that they are determined to get at him."

"What! Do you mean to say," said Butters, "that any one intends to nobble the Dancer?"

"So I hear, Joe; but not if we know it."

"Why, who's going to do it?"

"Never mind that," replied Gerald.

"The horse is all right. Now, you and I will keep watch here to-night, and take very good care they don't. If my information is correct we shall see who they are. It is gratifying in one way, at all events. It shows they think as highly of his chance as I do. Now be off and get something to eat as quick as you can, and then come back to me."

On Butters relieving guard Gerald slipped out on a similar errand, and on his return said, "Now, Joe, we shall have to pass the night here. You can lie down amongst the straw and go to sleep. I can trust you to stick to me in a row, but you know, Joe, I can't trust you to keep awake."

"Well, Mr. Rockingham, I've a way of dropping off, and the worst of it is I sleep that heavy that I take a good deal of waking."

"All right! you go and lie down.

Very little sleep does for me, and I'll get that towards morning. In the meanwhile, I'll keep watch."

That the spirit may be willing but the flesh weak is a very world-worn axiom, and to no one did it apply more forcibly than to Mr. Butters. He would spare himself in no wise to secure success and glory to Riddleton, but in the matter of watchfulness and abstinence he was frail. He could not keep awake by night nor abstain from the flesh-pots by day. He sighed over his somnolency and craving for pastry, and shuddered at the sight of a weighing-machine, but he knew his failings, and that to wrestle with them was beyond him. It was with a sigh of relief he heard the *rôle* assigned to him, and received his orders.

"You can depend upon me, Mr. Rockingham," said Joe, as he nestled down amongst the straw. "I a'nt good, perhaps, at keeping my eyes open, but I am all there when I am wanted. You can depend upon me, Mr. Rockingham. I'm all there, all, all," and here a low snore terminated Mr. Butters's protestations of fealty.

Gerald seated himself on the corn-bin, and commenced his vigil. With the big stake he had on the morrow, and accustomed to do with but little sleep, he felt no inclination to close his eyes. Could his cousin be such a scoundrel as actually to meditate laming or poisoning the Dancing Master, or had he such confidence in his old influence over Greyson as to feel sure that he could persuade him to scratch the horse? No, his first impression was right. Greyson had doubtless declined to do that, and Elliston had resolved to disable the horse before the race. Would he attempt this himself? Hardly. He doubtless could lay his hand upon plenty of instruments to do his bidding if they were only well paid for it.

Then his thoughts reverted upon the race to-morrow, and how he should ride it. "Yes," he muttered, "he's a free horse, and runs best in front. He's thrown in as far as the weight goes, and if he does his best I'm afraid of nothing. I'll come right through and strangle the lot." Suddenly there was a slight glimmer of light beneath the bottom of the door, and a low grating sound, as of some one softly trying the lock.

"A skeleton key," said Gerald to himself, as he slipped quietly off the corn-bin, and crouched down behind it.

The door opened, and two men entered; the first carried a dark lantern, the slide of which he drew cautiously back: the second, a short, pursy man, had a twitch in one hand, and a short stick, marvellously like a heavy office ruler, in the other.

"Hold the lantern," said Elliston, in a low whisper. "If I get the twitch on,

I'll make him shin-sore artistically; if not, I must lame him clumsily with one blow. Come on, it's the far box."

The two stole along towards the Dancing Master's box, and, as they did so, Gerald rose from behind the corn-bin and crept stealthily after them. Absorbed in their own villainy they failed to hear his cautious footsteps. Elliston's hand was on the latch of the box, Pearson just raising the lantern to assist his partner, when Gerald exclaimed quietly, "Drop that, Mr. Elliston."

For a second or two the confederates were so disconcerted by discovery that they stood paralysed and speechless; then with a savage execration Elliston rushed upon his cousin, and, before Gerald had time to jump back, struck him across the face with the twitch.

"Here, Joe — Joe — help!" shouted young Rockingham, as he grappled fiercely with his assailant.

But the attorney was now quite alive to the exigencies of the situation; it was quite clear to him that to disable Gerald and escape as speedily as might be was now the only chance of averting most unpleasant consequences. He dodged for a second or two round the two struggling men, and was about to aim a heavy blow at Gerald, when Butters, plunging into the fray, caused him to look to himself, and the short heavy stick descended sharply upon Joe's cranium, instead of young Rockingham's, stretching the former senseless on the ground. At this juncture Gerald wrenched himself clear of his antagonist, and immediately took advantage of his position to commence out-fighting, and administer a sharp left-hander between the eyes that sent Elliston reeling against the sides of Caterham's box. Taking in the state of things at once, Gerald sprang upon the attorney, and, before Pearson was quite aware of the attack, had snatched the stick from his hand. There was no time to be lost; Pearson threw down the lantern and made for the door, which his confederates had already gained. The diversion was successful; in his anxiety to possess himself of the lantern before harm should come from it, for Pearson had cast it perilously near the straw, Gerald neglected pursuit; and, when that necessary act was accomplished, came to the hasty conclusion that it was better to succour Butters and soothe the horses, already disturbed and uneasy at the unusual noise, than follow the fugitives, both of whom he had recognised.

CHAPTER XIV.

THE CAMBRIDGESHIRE.

THERE was great excitement at Newmarket in the course of the next morning, for, despite the precautions of Gerald, it had oozed out that there had been a daring attempt to get at the favourite during the night. Except to Greyson Gerald had breathed no word of his nocturnal adventure, and he had cautioned Butters to be equally reticent. Joe had held his tongue pretty fairly, still he but lamely explained his cut head, and had not the *sang froid* to emulate his companion's coolness, who, if questioned about how he came by the mark on his cheek, replied curtly, "No matter." In the betting world, both in London and at Newmarket, the rush to get on the Dancing Master was tremendous, and even staggered the Ring, cool as that philosophical body ordinarily is. The outlays of Sir Marmaduke and his followers, coupled with that of Lord Whitby, completely ran away with the public's own judgment. Notwithstanding the many disappointments the horse had occasioned them, they argued that the astute baronet would never have trusted him once more unless upon unexceptional grounds. It was rumoured that, although running in Greyson's name, he was still Sir Marmaduke's property, that he had run a tremendous trial, and was 7 lb. in front of Caterham. Then this was Lord Whitby's year; everything he touched came off, and decades of bad luck were being rapidly avenged. Backers are notoriously superstitious, and many of them much given to following a lucky jockey, a lucky horse, a lucky stable, or even coincidences. In 1869, when the followers of the cherry and black remembered that Sir Joseph Hawley had won the Derby in the years 1858 and 1859, and that he had won it again in 1868, what wonder they hardened their hearts and looked upon it that he was bound to win it twice running in each decade, and dashed down their money on unlucky Pero in consequence. Old horses allotted light weights have many times shown a marvellous recovery of their juvenile form in the Cambridgeshire, and for all these reasons combined the public went wild about the Dancing Master, and the fielders shortened their price hourly.

There were many old hands who had entrusted their money to Caterham, and many others whose eggs were in other baskets, men who could not get over the horse's uncertain temper, and were themselves no believers in his ultimate victory, yet they all agreed that such a red-hot favourite they never remembered in all their experience, and, though no doubt there were exceptions they could all point to, yet these red-hot favourites generally won, or, at the worst, made their opponents tremble in their shoes. So that even those cool, unprejudiced race-goers who were ranged against the self-willed grey had conceived a great respect for his chance. Then there was that now-announced fact that he was to be the gentleman jockey's mount; and that at once ranged all the women on his side; and if in our gradually advancing civilisation there are people so innocent as to believe that ladies of the present day, or, for the matter of that, of many days past, do not bet, the writer respects their simplicity, and would not willingly disturb such credulity.

"I don't know quite what to think of it all, Mr. Rockingham," said the trainer, as Gerald looked in at the stables, previous to cantering up to the course. "The Dancer's a little fretful, and snatched at his corn this morning in a fidgety, impatient manner that looks bad for his behaviour on the heath to-day. He's an excitable horse, and last night's row in his stable there's no doubt upset him a bit. As for Caterham, he's as cool as possible; he's one of the level-tempered sort that a salvo of artillery wouldn't disturb except for the moment. Then how are you yourself, sir? No sleep and a rough-and-tumble fight ain't a good preparation for a big race."

"I'm all right, Greyson, never fear. I'll ride as good a race to-day as ever I did. Mind, put that heavy double-reined snaffle on him as we settled; pet, coax, and keep him as quiet as you can. Don't saddle among the others, so as not to excite him, and I shall do as I told you—come right through with him; so if you don't see me playing follow-my-leader before we've gone a quarter of a mile you will understand the Dancer's got his own opinion and I've had to give in to it."

"Yes, Mr. Rockingham, you're right after all. Though you're to ride your own way to-day, it's coming back to pretty much the orders I gave you more than two years ago."

"I shall ride identically the same way, except that I understand the brute's mouth better, thanks to Dollie. Now I'm off."

"And I trust to Heaven, Mr. Rockingham, you'll win. I've borne the tyranny of these men for years, and done more dirty work for them than I care to think about. Pearson has had me in his debt so deep that I dare not disobey him, but it was Mr. Elliston who gave the orders always. I've broken with them now, and must stand the consequences, but, after last night's business, I should fancy they'll be rather shy of law-courts, or aught else."

" You're not likely to see them to-day; and, win or lose, depend upon it they'll never set foot on an English racecourse again. When Lord Whitby and Sir Marmaduke hear the story, Messrs. Elliston and Pearson will get warning with regard to Newmarket depend upon it. As for the rest, Greyson, if we're beaten, you'll worry through, never fear."

The trainer sat musing on the now, so to say, historic corn-bin, behind which Gerald had crouched the preceding night. " To think," he muttered, " that my daughter should be going to marry a real swell; and not only that, but the best horseman in England, and one of the finest, pluckiest young ones ever I ran across, high or low. Damme, if ever they persuade me into doing another ' shunt.' Well," he continued, rising, " it's getting about time we were off. Joe, you may get 'em out and walk 'em up to the Heath. If anybody's got two for the big race which look better than mine, I should just like to see 'em, that's all. I'm just going across the yard to get my hack, I shan't be five minutes; but mind, Joe, the Cambridgeshire horses you're never to leave till their jockeys are in the saddle."

Another quarter of an hour, and Greyson and his horses were leisurely wending their way to the Heath. There, of course, the wildest *canards* about the attempt " to get at the favourite " were current. The people just down from London were agog to hear all about it, for the report had been wired to town; but, though there were plenty of the sojourners at Newmarket only too delighted to relate their version of the affair, yet, as we know, the actual particulars were known only to three people, besides the delinquents, namely, Gerald, Butters, and Greyson.

But, if the peril the favourite had been in was involved in mystery, there was no doubt in the public mind that it had been successfully surmounted, and their anxiety to be on what one of the boldest of the sporting prophets had pronounced "the best thing of the year," waxed stronger every hour. For the backers had fairly tired out the fielders, and the leading members of the Ring, when asked, "What about the Dancing Master?" replied, "they'd no more money to lay." Still it had been a good betting race from the first, and, though there was no doubt the success of the Dancing Master would take an immense sum out of the Ring, there were a wonderful lot of whilsome favourites that had never even seen Newmarket, to assist them on settling day, to say nothing of various other public fancies, that money would have to be paid over largely should they go down before the favourite.

That the story of the attempt to get at the favourite should reach the ears of such strong supporters of his chance as Sir Marmaduke and Captain Farrington was only natural, and the baronet, upon arriving on the Heath, at once sought Gerald, with a view to hearing the true version of the affair, and also to learn from the best authority that the horse had really suffered no injury. Sir Marmaduke had backed the Dancing Master heavily, and it had been in consequence of what Gerald had told him. The baronet, with his great chum, Captain Farrington, had no sooner arrived at Newmarket than he was told "Jim Forrest" wished to see him, and Gerald then advised them both to try and get back their Hunt Cup losses over the Cambridgeshire. Sir Marmaduke at first demurred, and vowed he would never risk another shilling on that evil-tempered grey. But Gerald implored them both to have at all events a little on the Dancing Master this time.

"It's absurd, Sir Marmaduke, to say I lost you the Leger a year ago, but I have always bitterly regretted that I let my absurd false pride stand in the way, and begged off riding for you at Doncaster. Blackton is quite as good a man as I, and I've no doubt did the horse every justice, but, you see, he's just one of those queer brutes that might try for some one he knew, and refuse to do so otherwise. I've reason to think he'll run kind with me. I know he's very well, and I'll guarantee he's meant."

"All right, Rockingham, I'll have a quiet hundred on, and you'd better trust him once more, Marm, to that extent," said Farrington.

And so at last it was settled that the Dancing Master was to be once more entrusted with what Farrington described as a "modest century a-piece." But it was little likely that such two daring plungers would restrict their investments to that amount, and, as we know, Sir Marmaduke's operations at "the Rooms" had been conducted on his wonted scale. Lord Whitby also had derived his inspiration from the same source, so that "the Dancer" numbered amongst his supporters some of the very heaviest bettors on the turf.

But Gerald was by no means easy to come by, and Sir Marmaduke cantered his hack about a good deal in the fruitless endeavour to get speech with him. He was purposely keeping out of the way as much as possible. He was anxious to avoid all questioning about last night's work till the big race was over. He certainly now held his cousin in the hollow of his hand. Let him but denounce Cuthbert Elliston and Pearson to Sir Marmaduke and Lord Whitby, both members of the Jockey Club, and the pair were socially ruined. It would be bad enough for the attorney, but for Elliston it meant social extinction.

He had not quite made up his mind as to what he would do. To take a terrible revenge for all the woe he believed these two men to have wrought his father, to repay his cousin's undying enmity fourfold, all this was within his power; but, on the other hand, Elliston was his cousin, and the disgrace of one member of a family is a thing never to be desired by the rest, however they may dislike him or her.

Pearson also would make very easy terms with Greyson if he were once let know that silence about last night's business was conditional on his doing so. Gerald had so far seen neither of the confederates on the heath, still that might be because they were keeping aloof from the crowd as far as business permitted.

But, though Sir Marmaduke failed to

find Gerald, he at length discovered Greyson with his charges, walking quietly round and round, at the back of the Ditch.

"Good morning, Greyson," said the baronet. "What is all this I hear about an attempt to get at your horse last night?"

"Well, Sir Marmaduke, it didn't succeed, and we don't want to talk about it. I'm told you've backed my horse for a good bit. I can only say he never was better, and if he don't win to-day it's no fault of mine. He can't be fitter, but he's a bit of a rogue, as you know, and, though Mr. Rockingham thinks he'll run honest with him, I don't know what to think about it."

"He looks well, and so for the matter of that does Caterham. Then, Mr. Elliston fancies his chance very much, and, to tell you the truth, so do I, although I let Rockingham persuade me into backing the other."

"The two horses will run on their merits, Sir Marmaduke, and I've no doubt whatever that the grey *can* beat Caterham. Whether he *will* depends on himself."

By this time Butters and his assistants had whipped the rugs off, and were carefully preparing Caterham and the Dancer for the coming struggle, when Gerald cantered up on his hack.

"Weighed in?" said the trainer interrogatively.

"Yes," replied Gerald, "7·12; all right. Robinson and I stand a cross fifty on our mounts. Look sharp, Joe, and slip my saddle on to the back of the Dancer."

"Ah, he rides Caterham, and backs yours against his own as a hedge," replied the trainer. "Where is he?"

"Here he comes," replied Gerald, pointing to a horseman who was nearing them as fast as his steed could carry him.

"Good morning, Rockingham," said Sir Marmaduke. "I came down here to look for you, as I'm told you had a bit of trouble at the stables last night, but Greyson tells me you prefer to hold your tongue about it. I can only say that for such a thing to be possible is a slur upon Newmarket, and if you like to bring it forward I'm quite prepared to take it up."

"Thank you, Sir Marmaduke, but neither I nor the horse am any the worse, and we'll leave it alone for the present, at all events. I'm off now; but remember," he continued, dropping his voice, "if you see me in front at 'the turn of the lands' I shall take a deal of catching. —Now, Joe, give me a leg up. I want to have the Dancer to myself for a few minutes before we go down to the post. What's the latest news up there, Robinson?" and Gerald jerked his finger in the direction of the betting-ring.

"Yours as strong as brandy in the market, mine very steady; but that Fedora that won the Leger last year has come with a rattle, and there's apparently plenty of people who think she can give us 7 lbs. and lose us. They'll change their note before the day is over, eh, Jim?"

"You're safe to finish in front of her, Tom, and I shall beat you both, or not be in it at all. Now I'm off to give my mount a canter," and as he spoke Gerald, who was by this time in the saddle, set his horse quietly going in the direction of the Cambridgeshire post.

"Well, I shall go back to the stand to see the race," said the baronet. "Wish you success, Greyson," and sticking spurs to his hack Sir Marmaduke made the best of his way back to the desired coign of vantage.

"What orders, Mr. Greyson?" inquired Tom Robinson, when he found himself duly installed on Caterham's back.

"Mr. Elliston always gives his own

orders," rejoined the trainer, sharply. "If he hasn't seen you yet, no doubt he will at the starting-post."

"Supposing he don't?" inquired Robinson, curtly.

"Then ride him as you like. The horse can both race and stay, and is thoroughly wound up. I can tell you no more, and decline to give any orders under the circumstances."

"It ain't like Mr. Elliston," replied the jockey, as he cantered off to the post. "No," he muttered, "one's usually rather hampered with orders when one rides for him."

"Where are you going to see the race from, Marm?" inquired Captain Farrington, as the baronet cantered up to the betting-ring. "It's been pretty lively work in here for the last half-hour. The Dancing Master's nominally first favourite, but there's nobody has any money left to lay. Caterham's firm, and Fedora's come with a rattle, while half-a-dozen more are backed a bit."

"I'm going on to the stand, as I want to see how our horse gets off, and how he is when he passes it. I have just seen Rockingham. He means coming right through if he can, which will suit the Dancing Master's temper, and make the most of his light weight."

"All right; but we shan't see what wins from there."

"No, but young Rockingham says he shall have about won at the 'turn in the lands' just beyond."

"I like his extraordinary confidence, although I don't understand it, more especially with such a disappointing horse as he is riding," replied Farrington, as they took their places and adjusted their glasses.

The roar of the Ring is hushed, for the twenty-six horses are now in the hands of the starter, and speculation has ceased.

Greyson and Butters are both down at the post to see the Riddleton pair despatched on heir journey. There are some few false starts, and, though the Dancing Master behaves tolerably well, yet he gives more than one manifestation that the old Adam is by no manner of means dead within him. Still, when the flag does fall he gets off on very fair terms with his horses, and to Gerald's delight takes hold of his bridle as if he meant it. The first to show in front is a lightly-weighted four-year called St. Lawrence, but just before reaching the stand Gerald deprives him of the command, and at the "turn in the lands" is leading a couple of lengths.

"Looks rosy so far," said the baronet.

"Yes; but they're a long way off yet, not half way, indeed," rejoined Farrington.

In a fly nearly opposite the winning-post were Dollie and her mother, both in a state of considerable excitement, with their race-glasses riveted on the straight broad green ribbon that constitutes the Cambridge course.

"The favourite leads. The favourite walks in!" shout half a score of the Dancer's enthusiastic supporters.

"Caterham's going well, and Fedora's not done with," exclaims a veteran in the next carriage to Dollie. "But by Jove young Rockingham is bringing them along a cracker. Some of them won't last much longer. Looking at the tailing already."

"The mare's done with. Fedora's beat!" roar a hundred throats as the Leger victress succumbs to the severity of the pace.

"Robinson's riding Caterham!" yell the crowd again, as a couple of hundred yards from home that jockey is compelled to call upon his horse to keep his place.

"The favourite wins in a canter!" cry a score of voices. Ah, what's this in orange that's coming like a flash almost under the judge's chair? Does Forrest see it? He does evidently, but sits still as death. It is a supreme moment with Gerald. The Dancing Master he knows is doing pretty well his best. Dare he move on his horse? If he does, that eccentric animal may shut up instantaneously. The new comer on the scene has caught him, has reached his girths, is now at his head. Still Gerald sits immovable. They are within two or three strides of home, and the orange horseman is doing all he knows. "The Dancer wins!" "Lisette wins!" and as the two shoot past the post, Gerald still motionless, the crowd draw a long breath, and ask each other what's won?

"Forrest threw the race away," cries one indignant backer of the favourite; "he never even called on his horse."

"I tell you he's won, and never rode a more magnificent race," rejoins another.

"Wait till the numbers are up and you'll see," retorted the first.

Whichever way it was it was evidently a very close thing between the favourite and this almost friendless outsider, a mare who had started at the extreme price of 30 to 1, but whose six stone four had stood her in good stead, thanks to the severity of the pace.

Up go the numbers at last, and Gerald is as much relieved as anyone to find that his adversary failed to quite get up, and that the verdict is in his favour by a short head.

CHAPTER XV.

CONCLUSION.

THE announcement of the winner on the telegraph board was greeted with ominous silence. The Ring as a rule take their punishment without flinching, but men cannot be expected to wax hilarious over the losing of money. Then, again, Mr. Greyson was no popular owner of race-horses whose money the Ring had often had, but a chary backer, manager of a crafty, unscrupulous stable, that had set the fielders many a hard problem to solve, and bled them wickedly many a time. Even the public, who at the eleventh hour had rushed wildly on the Dancing Master, were dissatisfied. They had had to accept a very short price, and they had lost many and many a pound over the capricious winner when he had declined resolutely to gallop a yard for their investments. It was no doubt a wonderfully fine point between the leading pair, and Gerald frankly admitted he did not know whether he had just won or just lost till the numbers were up; but the decision of the judge on any leading English racecourse is no more disputed than the summing-up of a judge in any one of our law-courts. That there have been cases in which the turf verdict has been deemed a mistake, similarly as the summing-up at Westminster has been held erroneous, there is no doubt; but in neither case is it ever regarded as other than final.

"You were about right, Marm," said Farrington, when the result of the race reached them, " and so was Rockingham.

At 'the turn of the land' things looked very comfortable. It was the place for the Dancing Master's backers with the straight tip to see it from, but it must have been a wonderful squeak at the finish from all accounts."

"Yes; all our own fault," replied the baronet, sententiously. "We were dolts to forget that mare's form of last year. It's all right, but she was every bit as much turned loose as the Dancer."

"Oh, Gerald, my darling, I thought you had lost," exclaimed Dollie, as, the "weighing-in" satisfactorily concluded, Rockingham cantered up to his betrothed's carriage to receive her congratulations.

"I was much afraid so myself, and I fancy it was about as short a head as ever was given, but I was afraid to move on the Dancer. Good horse as he is, he was about all out, and I thought at any attempt to call upon him he would perhaps turn it up."

CONCLUSION. 273

"I don't think so myself," rejoined Dollie, "but that is mere matter of opinion. He ran better in the snaffle, didn't he?"

"Yes; and for all I know might have won much more decidedly if I had dared take any liberties with him. As it was I never interfered further than taking him to the front. I followed your father's original orders afterwards, and left it to himself."

"And the old horse was just equal to the occasion, eh, Gerald?"

"Yes; it was a shave, and I never rode so trying a race, and never shall by any possibility again. To have a wife and a home depending, so to speak, on the result, and nothing for it but to sit and suffer, is to test one's nerve and patience with a vengeance, and whether young Craddock had caught me or not I didn't know till I saw the numbers."

"Congratulations, Mr. Rockingham,"

said a deep voice behind them. "I have been indebted to your horsemanship a good many times this year, but anything finer than your masterly inactivity just now I never witnessed."

"Ah, Lord Whitby, it is a comfort to know you understood it. Half the people here think I all but lost the race from carelessness."

"Half the people here are chattering idiots," rejoined the irascible peer. "On a horse like that you were afraid, of course, to move."

"Let me introduce you to my wife that is to be," interposed Gerald, abruptly. He was in good humour with the world, and in no mood for any causeless explosion on the part of his irritable patron.

"Then I must still further congratulate you," rejoined Lord Whitby, as he raised his hat to Dollie, "and I trust your bride will accept a trifling memento of the Cambridgeshire from an old friend of your father's. Your intended excelled himself to-day. It was the most perfect exhibition of nerve and patience his winning the Cambridgeshire I have witnessed in five-and-thirty years' racing. May you both be sincerely happy," and once more raising his hat his lordship rode off.

It was a grim settling next Monday at Tattersall's. The Ring paid, as that often-abused body as a rule always does, but there was a heavy account due from the owner of Caterham, for the meeting of which apparently no provision whatever had been made. Mr. Elliston, it was rumoured, had gone abroad, nor could any one remember to have seen him since the day previous to the Cambridgeshire. Although Sam Pearson was not present, such bets as stood in his own name were all met, but the bookmakers felt pretty certain that he was actually responsible for a considerable portion of those made by his colleague, although his commissioner disclaimed any such liability on his part.

"Rather warm for the fraternity," remarked Farrington to Broughton, as he swept another little sheaf of banknotes into his hat.

"Yes, Captain, it's a scorcher, that's what it is, and Mr. Elliston not 'weighing-in' with the Caterham money of course makes it rather worse for us. Still, none of us grudge Lord Whitby, yourself, or Sir Marmaduke your winnings. We've hit you all hard enough in your time, and we don't generally whimper when we find 'you've got us on toast.'"

The bookmaker's language was perhaps enigmatical, but Farrington was thoroughly versed in the shibboleth of the Betting Ring, and manifested no surprise.

"Mr. Elliston's account not being to the fore is, of course, a little hard upon you, but I've no doubt it's only a question of time."

"Yes, I suppose so; Mr. Elliston's an old customer, if not a very liberal one, and I daresay he'll settle after a while."

But it was a long day before Cuthbert Elliston ventured to return to England, nor was his face ever seen again on an English racecourse. A hurried consultation took place between him and Pearson when they found themselves beyond the reach of pursuit, and they came to the conclusion that it behoved them to get away from Newmarket as speedily as possible, and they accordingly departed by the first train in the morning. When in the course of the afternoon the result of the race reached town, and Elliston ran over his betting-book, he found that he had stretched out his hand too far in his anxiety to grasp a large stake. It would be impossible for him to settle his liabilities in full, and he dared not besides face the consequences of his iniquitous attempt at disabling the favourite. The evening papers all alluded briefly to the affair, one with the addition that "it understood the most thorough investigation of the rascally business would take place, and it was much to be desired, in the best interests of the turf, that the prompters of the dastardly outrage should be dragged before the bar of public opinion, should evidence not be forthcoming to place them at the bar of a court of justice side by side of the miserable tools they had suborned."

Elliston crossed the Channel by that night's mail, while his partner sped northwards.

Gerald had a long talk with Greyson on the evening of the race, and finally they came to the determination to keep the affair to themselves.

"I owe my cousin no kindness, but it will not redound to the credit of the family to expose him. We have won, and can afford to be liberal, and, providing the pair of them make no attempt to set foot on a racecourse in future, we'll hold our tongues. Eh, Greyson?"

"Yes; I think it will be best," replied the trainer. "You see, I've got a good bit of money together now, and if you take Pearson in hand I have no doubt I can settle with him on reasonable terms."

The attorney was only too glad to purchase silence about a transaction which would irretrievably ruin him if promulgated, and made no fuss about striking off usurious interest from the trainer's liabilities. He further covenanted for both himself and his partner that they should retire from the Turf; and the sale of Phaeton, Caterham, &c., was speedily advertised. Nobody ever penetrated the cause of the abrupt break-up of the Elliston and Pearson confederacy, though Sir Marmaduke had a shrewd suspicion of the truth. It was usually attributed to an unsuccessful season, to which their severe losses over the Cambridgeshire put the coping-stone. As for the attorney, he throve and prospered exceedingly in his profession, and on the whole probably benefitted by his retirement from racing. With his partner it was different; he merely substituted the card-table for the racecourse, and frequented the chief play resorts of the Continent. As he encountered there many professional gamblers, with more skill, but quite as unscrupulous as himself, he continued in his usual state of irritable impecuniosity, and poor Mrs. Elliston dreed as hard a lot as it is posssible to mete out to woman.

Shortly after Christmas two weddings were celebrated in the parish church of Cranley; for Lord Whitby had acceded to Gerald's request to be allowed to buy the old place back from him.

"Certainly, my dear Rockingham," he said; "I don't want it. Take it at what I paid for it. I bought it chiefly to prevent that d——d scoundrel Cuthbert Elliston having it."

Ellen and Mrs. Rockingham had set their hearts upon the double ceremony taking place from Cranley, so the Greysons became Mrs. Rockingham's guests at the Chase for that week; and in the little village church, where they had knelt together as children, the brother and sister, one bright February morning, embarked upon the unknown waters of married life.

"Ah!" laughed Ellen to her sister-in-law, as the pair stood surveying their wedding presents, "how you and Gerald do beat us in this respect! It is better to marry a crack jockey than a poor parson when it comes to such jewels as these;" and Miss Rockingham lifted admiringly a handsome set of pearls and turquoise, the bridal gift of Lord Whitby.

*   *   *   *

There is no more to be told. All comedies finish with a marriage; and it is to be hoped that the old tag may apply: " that they lived happy ever afterwards." Gerald not only continued to follow his profession, but commenced the formation of a stud-farm at the Chase, and at the end of a few years the Cranley yearlings had earned for themselves a high reputation in the Doncaster sale-ring. He further usually had some few horses in training at Riddleton, with which he was more or less lucky.

In the hall of the Chase hangs a large picture of an almost snow-white steed, who has for years been lord of the Cranley stud, to whom Gerald always points as the horse who won back for him the lost home of his ancestors.

THE END.

www.ingramcontent.com/pod-product-compliance
Lightning Source LLC
Chambersburg PA
CBHW031337230426
43670CB00006B/363